A HANDBOOK OF STOIC PHILOSOPHY

HOW TO LIVE

THE ENCHIRIDION AND *DISCOURSES*

EPICTETUS

Translated by George Long

CLASSICS

Published 2025

FINGERPRINT! CLASSICS
Prakash Books

Fingerprint Publishing
@FingerprintP
@fingerprintpublishingbooks
www.fingerprintpublishing.com

ISBN: 978 93 6214 909 1

"Observe whom you yourself praise, when you praise many persons without partiality: do you praise the just or the unjust? The just. Whether do you praise the moderate or the immoderate? The moderate. And the temperate or the intemperate? The temperate. If then you make yourself such a person, you will know that you will make yourself beautiful; but so long as you neglect these things, you must be ugly, even though you contrive all you can to appear beautiful."

Very little is known of the life of Epictetus. It is said that he was a native of Hierapolis in Phrygia, a town between the Maeander and a branch of the Maeander named the Lycus. Hierapolis is mentioned in the epistle of Paul to the people of Colossae (Coloss. iv., 13); from which it has been concluded that there was a Christian church in Hierapolis in the time of the apostle. The date of the birth of Epictetus is unknown. The only recorded fact of his early life is that he was a slave in Rome, and his master was Epaphroditus, a profligate freedman of the Emperor Nero. There is a story that the master broke his slave's leg by torturing him; but it is better to trust to the evidence of Simplicius, the commentator on the *Enchiridion*, or Manual, who says that Epictetus was weak in body and lame from an early age. It is not said how he became a slave; but it has been asserted in modern times that the parents sold the child. I have not, however, found any authority for this statement.

It may be supposed that the young slave showed intelligence, for his master sent or permitted him to attend the lectures of C. Musonius Rufus, an eminent Stoic philosopher. It may seem strange that such a master should have wished to have his slave made into a philosopher; but Garnier, the author of a *Mémoire sur les Ouvrages d'Epictète*, explains this matter very well in a communication to Schweighaeuser. Garnier says: "Epictetus, born at Hierapolis of Phrygia of poor parents, was indebted apparently for the advantages of a good education to the whim, which was common at the end of the Republic and under the first emperors, among the great of Rome to reckon among their numerous slaves grammarians, poets, rhetoricians, and philosophers, in the same way as rich financiers in these later ages have been led to form at a great cost rich and numerous libraries. This supposition is the only one which can explain to us how a wretched child, born as poor as Irus, had received a good education, and how a rigid Stoic was the slave of Epaphroditus, one of the officers of the imperial guard. For we cannot suspect that it was through predilection for the Stoic doctrine, and for his own use, that the confidant and the minister of the debaucheries of Nero would have desired to possess such a slave."

Some writers assume that Epictetus was manumitted by his master, but I can find no evidence for this statement. Epaphroditus accompanied Nero when he fled from Rome before his enemies, and he aided the miserable tyrant in killing himself. Domitian (Sueton., Domit. 14), afterwards put Epaphroditus to death for this service to Nero. We may conclude that Epictetus in some way obtained his freedom, and that he began to teach at Rome; but after the expulsion of the philosophers from Rome by Domitian, A.D. 89, he retired to Nicopolis in Epirus, a city built by Augustus to commemorate the victory at Actium. Epictetus opened a school or lecture room at Nicopolis, where he taught till he was an old man. The time of his death is unknown. Epictetus was never married, as we learn from Lucian (Demonax, c. 55, torn, ii., ed. Hemsterh., p. 393). When Epictetus was finding fault with Demonax, and advising him to take a wife and beget children, for this also, as Epictetus said, was a philosopher's duty, to leave in place of himself another in the universe, Demonax refuted the doctrine by answering: Give me then, Epictetus, one of your own daughters. Simplicius says (Comment., c. 46, p. 432, ed. Schweigh.) that Epictetus lived alone a long time. At last he took a woman into his house as a nurse for a child, which one of Epictetus' friends was going to expose on account of his poverty, but Epictetus took the child and brought it up.

Photius (Biblioth., 58) mentions among Arrian's works *Conversations with Epictetus*, (Greek: *Homiliai Epichtaeton*), in twelve books. Upton thinks that this work is only another name for the Discourses, and that Photius has made the mistake of taking the Conversations to be a different work from the Discourses. Yet Photius has enumerated eight books of the Discourses and twelve books of the Conversations. Schweighaeuser observes that Photius had not seen these works of Arrian on Epictetus, for so he concludes from the brief notice of these works by Photius. The fact is that Photius does not say that he had read these books, as he generally does when he is speaking of the books which he enumerates in his Bibliotheca. The conclusion is that we are not certain that there was a work of Arrian entitled, *The Conversations of Epictetus*.

Upton remarks in a note on iii., 23 (p. 184, Trans.), that "there are many passages in these dissertations which are ambiguous or rather confused on account of the small questions, and because the matter is not expanded by oratorical copiousness, not to mention other causes." The discourses of Epictetus, it is supposed, were spoken extempore, and so one thing after another would come into the thoughts of the speaker (Wolf). Schweighaeuser also observes in a note (ii., 336 of his edition) that the connection of the discourse is sometimes obscure through the omission of some words which are necessary to indicate the connection of the thoughts. The reader then will find that he cannot always understand Epictetus, if he does not read him very carefully, and some passages more than once. He must also think and reflect, or he will miss the meaning. I do not say that the book is worth all this trouble. Every man must judge for himself. But I should not have translated the book, if I had not thought it worth study; and I think that all books of this kind require careful reading, if they are worth reading at all.

G.L.

CONTENTS

DISCOURSES

OF THE THINGS WHICH ARE IN OUR POWER AND NOT IN OUR POWER

Of all the faculties (except that which I shall soon mention), you will find not one which is capable of contemplating itself, and, consequently, not capable either of approving or disapproving. How far does the grammatic art possess the contemplating power? As far as forming a judgment about what is written and spoken. And how far music? As far as judging about melody. Does either of them then contemplate itself? By no means. But when you must write something to your friend, grammar will tell you what words you should write; but whether you should write or not, grammar will not tell you. And so it is with music as to musical sounds; but whether you should sing at the present time and play on the lute, or do neither, music will not tell you. What faculty then will tell you? That which contemplates both itself and all other things. And what is this faculty? The rational faculty; for this is the only faculty that we have received which examines itself, what it is, and what power it has, and what is the value of this gift, and examines all other faculties: for what else is there which tells us that golden things are beautiful, for they do not say so themselves? Evidently it is the faculty which is capable of judging of appearances. What else judges of music, grammar, and the other faculties, proves their uses, and points out the occasions for using them? Nothing else.

What then should a man have in readiness in such circumstances? What else than this? What is mine, and what is not mine; and what is permitted to me, and what is not permitted to me. I must die. Must I then die lamenting? I must be put in chains. Must I then also lament? I must go into exile. Does any man then hinder me from going with smiles and cheerfulness and contentment? Tell me the secret which you possess. I will not, for this is in my power. But I will put you in chains. Man, what are you talking about? Me, in chains? You may fetter my leg, but my will not even Zeus himself can overpower. I will throw you into prison. My poor body, you mean. I will cut your head off. When then have I told you that my head alone cannot be cut off? These are the things which philosophers should meditate on, which they should write daily, in which they should exercise themselves.

What then did Agrippinus say? He said, "I am not a hindrance to myself." When it was reported to him that his trial was going on in the Senate, he said: "I hope it may turn out well; but it is the fifth hour of the day"—this was the time when he was used to exercise himself and then take the cold bath—"let us go and take our exercise." After he had taken his exercise, one comes and tells him, "You have been condemned." "To banishment," he replies, "or to death?" "To banishment." "What about my property?" "It is not taken from you." "Let us go to Aricia then," he said, "and dine."

HOW A MAN ON EVERY OCCASION CAN MAINTAIN HIS PROPER CHARACTER

To the rational animal only is the irrational intolerable; but that which is rational is tolerable. Blows are not naturally intolerable. How is that? See how the Lacedaemonians endure whipping when they have learned that whipping is consistent with reason. To hang yourself is not intolerable. When then you have the opinion that it is rational, you go and hang yourself. In short, if we observe, we shall find that the animal man is pained by nothing so much as by that which is irrational; and, on the contrary, attracted to nothing so much as to that which is rational.

Only consider at what price you sell your own will: if for no other reason, at least for this, that you sell it not for a small sum. But that which is great and superior perhaps belongs to Socrates and such as are like him. Why then, if we are naturally such, are not a very great number of us like him? Is it true then that all horses become swift, that all dogs are skilled in tracking footprints? What then, since I am naturally dull, shall I, for this reason, take no pains? I hope not. Epictetus is not superior to

Socrates; but if he is not inferior, this is enough for me; for I shall never be a Milo, and yet I do not neglect my body; nor shall I be a Croesus, and yet I do not neglect my property; nor, in a word, do we neglect looking after anything because we despair of reaching the highest degree.

HOW A MAN SHOULD PROCEED FROM THE PRINCIPLE OF GOD BEING THE FATHER OF ALL MEN TO THE REST

If a man should be able to assent to this doctrine as he ought, that we are all sprung from God in an especial manner, and that God is the father both of men and of gods, I suppose that he would never have any ignoble or mean thoughts about himself. But if Caesar (the emperor) should adopt you, no one could endure your arrogance; and if you know that you are the son of Zeus, will you not be elated? Yet we do not so; but since these two things are mingled in the generation of man, body in common with the animals, and reason and intelligence in common with the gods, many incline to this kinship, which is miserable and mortal; and some few to that which is divine and happy. Since then it is of necessity that every man uses everything according to the opinion which he has about it, those, the few, who think that they are formed for fidelity and modesty and a sure use of appearances have no mean or ignoble thoughts about themselves; but with the many it is quite the contrary. For they say, What am I? A poor, miserable man, with my wretched bit of flesh. Wretched, indeed; but you possess something better than your bit of flesh. Why then do you neglect that which is better, and why do you attach yourself to this?

Through this kinship with the flesh, some of us inclining to it become like wolves, faithless and treacherous and mischievous; some become like lions, savage and bestial and untamed; but the greater part of us become foxes, and other worse animals. For what else is a slanderer and malignant man than a fox, or some other more wretched and meaner animal? See then and take care that you do not become some one of these miserable things.

OF PROGRESS OR IMPROVEMENT

He who is making progress, having learned from philosophers that desire means the desire of good things, and aversion means aversion from bad things; having learned too that happiness and tranquillity are not attainable by man otherwise than by not failing to obtain what he desires, and not falling into that which he would avoid; such a man takes from himself desire altogether and confers it, but he employs his aversion only on things which are dependent on his will. For if he attempts to avoid anything independent of his will, he knows that sometimes he will fall in with something which he wishes to avoid, and he will be unhappy. Now if virtue promises good fortune and tranquillity and happiness, certainly also the progress towards virtue is progress towards each of these things. For it is always true that to whatever point the perfecting of anything leads us, progress is an approach towards this point.

How then do we admit that virtue is such as I have said, and yet seek progress in other things and make a display of it? What is the product of virtue? Tranquillity. Who then makes improvement? Is it he who has read many books of Chrysippus?

But does virtue consist in having understood Chrysippus? If this is so, progress is clearly nothing else than knowing a great deal of Chrysippus. But now we admit that virtue produces one thing, and we declare that approaching near to it is another thing, namely, progress or improvement. Such a person, says one, is already able to read Chrysippus by himself. Indeed, sir, you are making great progress. What kind of progress? But why do you mock the man? Why do you draw him away from the perception of his own misfortunes? Will you not show him the effect of virtue that he may learn where to look for improvement? Seek it there, wretch, where your work lies. And where is your work? In desire and in aversion, that you may not be disappointed in your desire, and that you may not fall into that which you would avoid; in your pursuit and avoiding, that you commit no error; in assent and suspension of assent, that you be not deceived. The first things, and the most necessary are those which I have named. But if with trembling and lamentation you seek not to fall into that which you avoid, tell me how you are improving.

Do you then show me your improvement in these things? If I were talking to an athlete, I should say, Show me your shoulders; and then he might say, Here are my Halteres. You and your Halteres look to that. I should reply, I wish to see the effect of the Halteres. So, when you say: Take the treatise on the active powers (Greek: *hormea*), and see how I have studied it, I reply: Slave, I am not inquiring about this, but how you exercise pursuit and avoidance, desire and aversion, how you design and purpose and prepare yourself, whether conformably to nature or not. If conformably, give me evidence of it, and I will say that you are making progress; but if not conformably, be gone, and not only expound your books, but write such books yourself; and what will you gain by it? Do you not know that the whole book costs only five denarii? Does then the expounder seem to be worth more than five denarii? Never then look for the matter itself in one place, and progress towards it in another. Where then is progress? If any of you, withdrawing himself from externals, turns to his own will (Greek: *proairesis*) to exercise it and to improve it by labor, so as to make it conformable to nature, elevated, free, unrestrained, unimpeded, faithful, modest; and if he has learned that he who desires or avoids the things which are not in his power can neither be faithful nor free, but of necessity he must change with them and be tossed about with them as in a tempest, and of necessity must subject himself to others who have the power to procure or prevent what lie desires or would avoid; finally, when he rises in the morning, if he observes and keeps these rules, bathes as a man of fidelity, eats as a modest man; in like manner, if in every matter that occurs he works out his chief principles (Greek: *ta proaegoumena*) as the runner does with reference to running, and the trainer of the voice with reference to the voice—this is the man who truly makes progress, and this is the man who has not travelled in vain. But if he has strained his efforts to the practice of reading books, and labors only at this, and has travelled for this, I tell him to return home immediately, and not to neglect his affairs there; for this for which he has travelled is nothing. But the other thing is something, to study how a man can rid his life of lamentation and groaning, and saying, Woe to me, and wretched that I am, and to rid it also of misfortune and disappointment, and to learn what death is, and exile, and prison, and poison, that he may be able to say when he is in fetters, Dear Crito, if it is the will of the gods that it be so, let it be so; and not to say, Wretched am I, an old man: have I kept my gray hairs for this? Who is it that speaks thus? Do you think that I shall name some man of no repute and of low condition? Does not Priam say this? Does not Oedipus say this? Nay, all kings say it! For what else is tragedy than the perturbations (Greek: *pathae*) of men who value externals exhibited in this kind of poetry? But if a man must learn by fiction that no external things which are independent of the will concern us, for my part I should like this fiction, by the aid of which I should live happily and undisturbed. But you must consider for yourselves what you wish.

What then does Chrysippus teach us? The reply is, to know that these things are not false, from which happiness comes and tranquillity arises. Take my books, and you will learn how true and conformable to nature are the things which make me free from perturbations. O great good fortune! O the great benefactor who points out the way! To Triptolemus all men have erected temples and altars, because he gave us food by cultivation; but to him who discovered truth and brought it to light and communicated it to all, not the truth which shows us how to live, but how to live well, who of you for this reason has built an altar, or a temple, or has dedicated a statue, or who worships God for this? Because the gods have given the vine, or wheat, we sacrifice to them; but because they have produced in the human mind that fruit by which they designed to show us the truth which relates to happiness, shall we not thank God for this?

AGAINST THE ACADEMICS

If a man, said Epictetus, opposes evident truths, it is not easy to find arguments by which we shall make him change his opinion. But this does not arise either from the man's strength or the teacher's weakness; for when the man, though he has been confuted, is hardened like a stone, how shall we then be able to deal with him by argument?

Now there are two kinds of hardening, one of the understanding, the other of the sense of shame, when a man is resolved not to assent to what is manifest nor to desist from contradictions. Most of us are afraid of mortification of the body, and would contrive all means to avoid such a thing, but we care not about the soul's mortification. And indeed with regard to the soul, if a man be in such a state as not to apprehend anything, or understand at all, we think that he is in a bad condition; but if the sense of shame and modesty are deadened, this we call even power (or strength).

OF PROVIDENCE

From everything, which is or happens in the world, it is easy to praise Providence, if a man possesses these two qualities: the faculty of seeing what belongs and happens to all persons and things, and a grateful disposition. If he does not possess these two qualities, one man will not see the use of things which are and which happen: another will not be thankful for them, even if he does know them. If God had made colors, but had not made the faculty of seeing them, what would have been their use? None at all. On the other hand, if he had made the faculty of vision, but had not made objects such as to fall under the faculty, what in that case also would have been the use of it? None at all. Well, suppose that he had made both, but had not made light? In that case, also, they would have been of no use. Who is it then who has fitted this to that and that to this?

What, then, are these things done in us only? Many, indeed, in us only, of which the rational animal had peculiar need; but you will find many common to us with irrational animals. Do they then understand what is done? By no means. For use is one thing, and understanding is another; God had need of irrational animals to make use of appearances, but of us to understand the use of appearances. It is therefore enough for them to eat and to drink, and to copulate, and to do all the other things which they severally do. But for us, to whom he has given also the intellectual faculty, these things are not sufficient; for unless we act in a proper and orderly manner, and conformably to the nature and constitution of each thing, we shall never attain our true end. For where the constitutions of living beings are different, there also the acts and the ends are different. In those animals then whose constitution is adapted only to use, use alone is enough; but in an animal (man), which has also the power of understanding the use, unless there be the due exercise of the understanding, he will never attain his proper end. Well then God constitutes every animal, one to be eaten, another to serve for agriculture, another to supply cheese, and another for some like use; for which purposes what need is there to understand appearances and to be able to distinguish them? But God has introduced man to be a spectator of God and of his works; and not only a spectator of them, but an interpreter. For this reason it is shameful for man to begin and to end where irrational animals do; but rather he ought to begin where they begin, and to end where nature ends in us; and nature ends in contemplation and understanding, and in a way of life conformable to nature. Take care then not to die without having been spectators of these things.

But you take a journey to Olympia to see the work of Phidias, and all of you think it a misfortune to die without having seen such things. But when there is no need to take a journey, and where a man is, there he has the works (of God) before him, will you not desire to see and understand them? Will you not perceive either what you are, or what you were born for, or what this is for which you have received the faculty of sight? But you may say, There are some things disagreeable and troublesome in life. And are there none at Olympia? Are you not scorched? Are you not pressed by a crowd? Are you not without comfortable means of bathing? Are you not wet when it rains? Have you not abundance of noise, clamor, and other disagreeable things? But I suppose that setting all these things off against the magnificence of the spectacle, you bear and endure. Well then and have you not received faculties by which you will be able to bear all that happens? Have you not received greatness of soul? Have you not received manliness? Have you not received endurance? And why do I trouble myself about anything that can happen if I possess greatness of soul? What shall distract my mind, or disturb me, or appear painful? Shall I not use the power for the purposes for which I received it, and shall I grieve and lament over what happens?

Come, then, do you also having observed these things look to the faculties which you have, and when you have looked at them, say: Bring now, O Zeus, any difficulty that thou pleasest, for I have means given to me by thee and powers for honoring myself through the things which happen. You do not so; but you sit still, trembling for fear that some things will happen, and weeping, and lamenting, and groaning for what does happen; and then you blame the gods. For what is the consequence of such meanness of spirit but impiety? And yet God has not only given us these faculties, by which we shall be able to bear everything that happens without being depressed or broken by it; but, like a good king and a true father, He has given us these faculties free from hindrance, subject to no compulsion, unimpeded, and has put them entirely in our own power, without even having reserved to Himself any power of hindering or impeding. You, who have received these powers free and as your own, use them not; you do not even see what you have received, and from whom; some of you being blinded to the giver, and not even acknowledging your benefactor, and others, through meanness of spirit, betaking yourselves to fault-finding and making charges against God. Yet I will show to you that you have powers and means for greatness of soul and manliness; but what powers you have for finding fault making accusations, do you show me.

HOW FROM THE FACT THAT WE ARE AKIN TO GOD A MAN MAY PROCEED TO THE CONSEQUENCES

I indeed think that the old man ought to be sitting here, not to contrive how you may have no mean thoughts nor mean and ignoble talk about yourselves, but to take care that there be not among us any young men of such a mind, that when they have recognized their kinship to God, and that we are fettered by these bonds, the body, I mean, and its possessions, and whatever else on account of them is necessary to us for the economy and commerce of life, they should intend to throw off these things as if they were burdens painful and intolerable, and to depart to their kinsmen. But this is the labor that your teacher and instructor ought to be employed upon, if he really were what he should be. You should come to him and say: Epictetus, we can no longer endure being bound to this poor body, and feeding it, and giving it drink and rest, and cleaning it, and for the sake of the body complying with the wishes of these and of those. Are not these things indifferent and nothing to us; and is not death no evil? And are we not in a manner kinsmen of God, and did we not come from him? Allow us to depart to the place from which we came; allow us to be released at last from these bonds by which we are bound and weighed down. Here there are robbers and thieves and courts of justice, and those who are named tyrants, and think that they have some power over us by means of the body and its possessions. Permit us to show them that they have no power over any man. And I on my part would say: Friends, wait for God: when he shall give the signal and release you from this service, then go to him; but for the present endure to dwell in this place where he has put you. Short indeed is this time of your dwelling here, and easy to bear for those who are so disposed; for what tyrant, or what thief, or what courts of justice are formidable to those who have thus considered as things of no value the body and the possessions of the body? Wait then, do not depart without a reason.

OF CONTENTMENT

With respect to gods, there are some who say that a divine being does not exist; others say that it exists, but is inactive and careless, and takes no forethought about anything; a third class say that such a being exists and exercises forethought, but only about great things and heavenly things, and about nothing on the earth; a fourth class say that a divine being exercises forethought both about things on the earth and heavenly things, but in a general way only, and not about things severally. There is a fifth class to whom Ulysses and Socrates belong, who say:

I move not without thy knowledge.—*Iliad*, x., 278.

Before all other things then it is necessary to inquire about each of these opinions, whether it is affirmed truly or not truly. For if there are no gods, how is it our proper end to follow them? And if they exist, but take no care of anything, in this case also how will it be right to follow them? But if indeed they do exist and look after things, still if there is nothing communicated from them to men, nor in fact to myself, how even so is it right (to follow them)? The wise and good man then, after considering all these things, submits his own mind to him who administers the whole, as good citizens do to the law of the state. He who is receiving instruction ought to come to be instructed with this intention, How shall I follow the gods in all things, how shall I be contented with the divine administration, and how can I become free? For he is free to whom everything happens according to his will, and whom no man can hinder. What then, is freedom madness? Certainly not; for madness and freedom do not consist. But, you say, I would have everything result just as I like, and in whatever way I like. You are mad, you are beside yourself. Do you not know that freedom is a noble and valuable thing? But for me inconsiderately to wish for things to happen as I inconsiderately like, this appears to be not only not noble, but even most base. For how do we proceed in the matter of writing? Do I wish to write the name of Dion as I choose? No, but I am taught to choose to write it as it ought to be written. And how with respect to music? In the same manner. And what universally in every art or science? Just the same. If it were not so, it would be of no value to know anything, if knowledge were adapted to every man's whim. Is it then in this alone, in this which is the greatest and the chief thing, I mean freedom, that I am permitted to will inconsiderately? By no means; but to be instructed is this, to learn to wish that everything may happen as it does. And how do things happen? As the disposer has disposed them? And he has appointed summer and winter, and abundance and scarcity, and virtue and vice, and all such opposites for the harmony of the whole; and to each of us he has given a body, and parts of the body, and possessions, and companions.

What then remains, or what method is discovered of holding commerce with them? Is there such a method by which they shall do what seems fit to them, and we not the less shall be in a mood which is conformable to nature? But you are unwilling to endure, and are discontented; and if you are alone, you call it solitude; and if you are with men, you call them knaves and robbers; and you find fault with your own parents and children, and brothers and neighbors. But you ought when you are alone to call this condition by the name of tranquillity and freedom, and to think yourself like to the gods; and when you are with many, you ought not to call it crowd, nor trouble, nor uneasiness, but festival and assembly, and so accept all contentedly.

What then is the punishment of those who do not accept? It is to be what they are. Is any person dissatisfied with being alone? Let him be alone. Is a man dissatisfied with his parents? Let him be a bad son, and lament. Is he dissatisfied with his children? Let him be a bad father. Cast him into prison. What prison? Where he is already, for he is there against his will; and where a man is against his will, there he is in prison. So Socrates was not in prison, for he was there willingly. Must my leg then be lamed? Wretch, do you then on account of one poor leg find fault with the world? Will you not willingly surrender it for the whole? Will you not withdraw from it? Will you not gladly part with it to him who gave it? And will you be vexed and discontented with the things established by Zeus, which he, with the Moirae (fates) who were present and spinning the thread of your generation, defined and put in order? Know you not how small a part you are compared with the whole. I mean with respect to the body, for as to intelligence you are not inferior to the gods nor less; for the magnitude of intelligence is not measured by length nor yet by height, but by thoughts.

HOW EVERYTHING MAY BE DONE ACCEPTABLY TO THE GODS

When some one asked, How may a man eat acceptably to the gods, he answered: If he can eat justly and contentedly, and with equanimity, and temperately, and orderly, will it not be also acceptable to the gods? But when you have asked for warm water and the slave has not heard, or if he did hear has brought only tepid water, or he is not even found to be in the house, then not to be vexed or to burst with passion, is not this acceptable to the gods? How then shall a man endure such persons as this slave? Slave yourself, will you not bear with your own brother, who has Zeus for his progenitor, and is like a son from the same seeds and of the same descent from above? But if you have been put in any such higher place, will you immediately make yourself a tyrant? Will you not remember who you are, and whom you rule? That they are kinsmen, that they are brethren by nature, that they are the offspring of Zeus? But I have purchased them, and they have not purchased me. Do you see in what direction you are looking, that it is towards the earth, towards the pit, that it is towards these wretched laws of dead men? but towards the laws of the gods you are not looking.

WHAT PHILOSOPHY PROMISES

When a man was consulting him how he should persuade his brother to cease being angry with him, Epictetus replied: Philosophy does not propose to secure for a man any external thing. If it did (or if it were not, as I say), philosophy would be allowing something which is not within its province. For as the carpenter's material is wood, and that of the statuary is copper, so the matter of the art of living is each man's life. When then is my brother's? That again belongs to his own art; but with respect to yours, it is one of the external things, like a piece of land, like health, like reputation. But Philosophy promises none of these. In every circumstance I will maintain, she says, the governing part conformable to nature. Whose governing part? His in whom I am, she says.

How then shall my brother cease to be angry with me? Bring him to me and I will tell him. But I have nothing to say to you about his anger.

When the man who was consulting him said, I seek to know this, How, even if my brother is not reconciled to me, shall I maintain myself in a state conformable to nature? Nothing great, said Epictetus, is produced suddenly, since not even the grape or the fig is. If you say to me now that you want a fig, I will answer to you that it requires time: let it flower first, then put forth fruit, and then ripen. Is then the fruit of a fig-tree not perfected suddenly and in one hour, and would you possess the fruit of a man's mind in so short a time and so easily? Do not expect it, even if I tell you.

THAT WE OUGHT NOT TO BE ANGRY WITH THE ERRORS (FAULTS) OF OTHERS

Ought not then this robber and this adulterer to be destroyed? By no means say so, but speak rather in this way: This man who has been mistaken and deceived about the most important things, and blinded, not in the faculty of vision which distinguishes white and black, but in the faculty which distinguishes good and bad, should we not destroy him? If you speak thus you will see how inhuman this is which you say, and that it is just as if you would say, Ought we not to destroy this blind and deaf man? But if the greatest harm is the privation of the greatest things, and the greatest thing in every man is the will or choice such as it ought to be, and a man is deprived of this will, why are you also angry with him? Man, you ought not to be affected contrary to nature by the bad things of another. Pity him rather; drop this readiness to be offended and to hate, and these words which the many utter: "These accursed and odious fellows." How have you been made so wise at once? and how are you so peevish? Why then are we angry? Is it because we value so much the things of which these men rob us? Do not admire your clothes, and then you will not be angry with the thief. Consider this matter thus: you have fine clothes; your neighbor has not; you have a window; you wish to air the clothes. The thief does not know wherein man's good consists, but he thinks that it consist in having fine clothes, the very thing which you also think. Must he not then come and take them away? When you show a cake to greedy persons, and swallow it all yourself, do you expect them not to snatch it from you? Do not provoke them; do not have a window; do not air your clothes. I also lately had an iron lamp placed by the side of my household gods; hearing a noise at the door, I ran down, and found that the lamp had been carried off. I reflected that he who had taken the lamp had done nothing strange. What then? To-morrow, I said, you will find an earthen lamp; for a man only loses that which he has. I have lost my garment. The reason is that you had a garment. I have a pain in my head. Have you any pain in your horns? Why then are you troubled? For we only lose those things, we have only pains about those things, which we possess.

But the tyrant will chain—what? The leg. He will take away—what? The neck. What then will he not chain and not take away? The will. This is why the ancients taught the maxim, Know thyself. Therefore we ought to exercise ourselves in small things, and beginning with them to proceed to the greater. I have pain in the head. Do not say, Alas! I have pain in the ear. Do not say alas! And I do not say that you are not allowed to groan, but do not groan inwardly; and if your slave is slow in bringing a bandage, do not cry out and torment yourself, and say, Every body hates me; for who would not hate such a man? For the future, relying on these opinions, walk about upright, free; not trusting to the size of your body, as an athlete, for a man ought not to be invincible in the way that an ass is.

HOW WE SHOULD BEHAVE TO TYRANTS

If a man possesses any superiority, or thinks that he does when he does not, such a man, if he is uninstructed, will of necessity be puffed up through it. For instance, the tyrant says, I am master of all! And what can you do for me? Can you give me desire which shall have no hindrance? How can you? Have you the infallible power of avoiding what you would avoid? Have you the power of moving towards an object without error? And how do you possess this power? Come, when you are in a ship, do you trust to yourself or to the helmsman? And when you are in a chariot, to whom do you trust but to the driver? And how is it in all other arts? Just the same. In what, then, lies your power? All men pay respect to me. Well, I also pay respect to my platter, and I wash it and wipe it; and for the sake of my oil-flask, I drive a peg into the wall. Well, then, are these things superior to me? No, but they supply some of my wants, and for this reason I take care of them. Well, do I not attend to my ass? Do I not wash his feet? Do I not clean him? Do you not know that every man has regard to himself, and to you just the same as he has regard to his ass? For who has regard to you as a man? Show me. Who wishes to become like you? Who imitates you, as he imitates Socrates? But I can cut off your head. You say right. I had forgotten that I must have regard to you, as I would to a fever and the bile, and raise an altar to you, as there is at Rome an altar to fever.

What is it then that disturbs and terrifies the multitude? Is it the tyrant and his guards? (By no means.) I hope that it is not so. It is not possible that what is by nature free can be disturbed by anything else, or hindered by any other thing than by itself. But it is a man's own opinions which disturb him. For when the tyrant says to a man, I will chain your leg, he who values his leg says, Do not; have pity. But he who values his own will says, If it appears more advantageous to you, chain it. Do you not care? I do not care. I will show you that I am master. You cannot do that. Zeus has set me free; do you think that he intended to allow his own son to be enslaved? But you are master of my carcase; take it. So when you approach me, you have no regard to me? No, but I have regard to myself; and if you wish me to say that I have regard to you also, I tell you that I have the same regard to you that I have to my pipkin.

What then? When absurd notions about things independent of our will, as if they were good and (or) bad, lie at the bottom of our opinions, we must of necessity pay regard to tyrants: for I wish that men would pay regard to tyrants only, and not also to the bedchamber men. How is it that the man becomes all at once wise, when Caesar has made him superintendent of the close stool? How is it that we say immediately, Felicion spoke sensibly to me? I wish he were ejected from the bedchamber, that he might again appear to you to be a fool.

Has a man been exalted to the tribuneship? All who meet him offer their congratulations; one kisses his eyes, another the neck, and the slaves kiss his hands. He goes to his house, he finds torches lighted. He ascends the Capitol; he offers a sacrifice on the occasion. Now who ever sacrificed for having had good desires? for having acted conformably to nature? For in fact we thank the gods for those things in which we place our good.

A person was talking to me to-day about the priesthood of Augustus. I say to him: Man, let the thing alone; you will spend much for no purpose. But he replies, Those who draw up agreements will write my name. Do you then stand by those who read them, and say to such persons, It is I whose name is written there? And if you can now be present on ail such occasions, what will you do when you are dead? My name will remain. Write it on a stone, and it will remain. But come, what remembrance of you will there be beyond Nicopolis? But I shall wear a crown of gold. If you desire a crown at all, take a crown of roses and put it on, for it will be more elegant in appearance.

AGAINST THOSE WHO WISH TO BE ADMIRED

When a man holds his proper station in life, he does not gape after things beyond it. Man, what do you wish to happen to you? I am satisfied if I desire and avoid conformably to nature, if I employ movements towards and from an object as I am by nature formed to do, and purpose and design and assent. Why then do you strut before us as if you had swallowed a spit? My wish has always been that those who meet me should admire me, and those who follow me should exclaim, O the great philosopher! Who are they by whom you wish to be admired? Are they not those of whom you are used to say that they are mad? Well, then, do you wish to be admired by madmen?

ON PRAECOGNITIONS

Praecognitions are common to all men, and praecognition is not contradictory to praecognition. For who of us does not assume that Good is useful and eligible, and in all circumstances that we ought to follow and pursue it? And who of us does not assume that Justice is beautiful and becoming? When then does the contradiction arise? It arises in the adaptation of the praecognitions to the particular cases. When one man says, "He has done well; he is a brave man," and another says, "Not so; but he has acted foolishly," then the disputes arise among men. This is the dispute among the Jews and the Syrians and the Egyptians and the Romans; not whether holiness should be preferred to all things and in all cases should be pursued, but whether it is holy to eat pig's flesh or not holy. You will find this dispute also between Agamemnon and Achilles; for call them forth. What do you say, Agamemnon? ought not that to be done which is proper and right? "Certainly." Well, what do you say, Achilles? do you not admit that what is good ought to be done? "I do most certainly." Adapt your praecognitions then to the present matter. Here the dispute begins. Agamemnon says, "I ought not to give up Chryseis to her father." Achilles says, "You ought." It is certain that one of the two makes a wrong adaptation of the praecognition of "ought" or "duty." Further, Agamemnon says, "Then if I ought to restore Chryseis, it is fit that I take his prize from some of you." Achilles replies, "Would you then take her whom I love?" "Yes, her whom you love." "Must I then be the only man who goes without a prize? and must I be the only man who has no prize?" Thus the dispute begins.

What then is education? Education is the learning how to adapt the natural praecognitions to the particular things conformably to nature; and then to distinguish that of things some are in our power, but others are not. In our power are will and all acts which depend on the will; things not in our power are the body, the parts of the body, possessions, parents, brothers, children, country, and, generally, all with whom we live in society. In what then should we place the good? To what kind of things (Greek: *ousia*) shall we adapt it? To the things which are in our power? Is not health then a good thing, and soundness of limb, and life, and are not children and parents and country? Who will tolerate you if you deny this?

Let us then transfer the notion of good to these things. Is it possible, then, when a man sustains damage and does not obtain good things, that he can be happy? It is not possible. And can he maintain towards society a proper behavior? He can not. For I am naturally formed to look after my own interest. If it is my interest to have an estate in land, it is my interest also to take it from my neighbor. If it is my interest to have a garment, it is my interest also to steal it from the bath. This is the origin of wars, civil commotions, tyrannies, conspiracies. And how shall I be still able to maintain my duty towards Zeus? For if I sustain damage and am unlucky, he takes no care of me. And what is he to me if he cannot help me? And further, what is he to me if he allows me to be in the condition in which I am? I now begin to hate him. Why then do we build temples, why setup statues to Zeus, as well as to evil demons, such as to Fever; and how is Zeus the Saviour, and how the giver of rain, and the giver of fruits? And in truth if we place the nature of Good in any such things, all this follows.

What should we do then? This is the inquiry of the true philosopher who is in labor. Now I do not see what the good is nor the bad. Am I not mad? Yes. But suppose that I place the good somewhere among the things which depend on the will; all will laugh at me. There will come some greyhead wearing many gold rings on his fingers, and he will shake his head and say: "Hear, my child. It is right that you should philosophize; but you ought to have some brains also; all this that you are doing is silly. You learn the syllogism from philosophers; but you know how to act better than philosophers do." Man why then do you blame me, if I know? What shall I say to this slave? If I am silent, he will burst. I must speak in this way: "Excuse me, as you would excuse lovers; I am not my own master; I am mad."

HOW WE SHOULD STRUGGLE WITH CIRCUMSTANCES

It is circumstances (difficulties) which show what men are. Therefore when a difficulty falls upon you, remember that God, like a trainer of wrestlers, has matched you with a rough young man. For what purpose? you may say. Why, that you may become an Olympic conqueror; but it is not accomplished without sweat. In my opinion no man has had a more profitable difficulty than you have had, if you choose to make use of it as an athlete would deal with a young antagonist. We are now sending a scout to Rome; but no man sends a cowardly scout, who, if he only hears a noise and sees a shadow anywhere, comes running back in terror and reports that the enemy is close at hand. So now if you should come and tell us: "Fearful is the state of affairs at Rome; terrible is death; terrible is exile; terrible is calumny; terrible is poverty; fly, my friends, the enemy is near," we shall answer: "Begone, prophesy for yourself; we have committed only one fault, that we sent such a scout."

Diogenes, who was sent as a scout before you, made a different report to us. He says that death is no evil, for neither is it base; he says that fame (reputation) is the noise of madmen. And what has this spy said about pain, about pleasure, and about poverty? He says that to be naked is better than any purple robe, and to sleep on the bare ground is the softest bed; and he gives as a proof of each thing that he affirms his own courage, his tranquillity, his freedom, and the healthy appearance and compactness of his body. There is no enemy near, he says; all is peace. How so, Diogenes? "See,". he replies, "if I am struck, if I have been wounded, if I have fled from any man." This is what a scout ought to be. But you come to us and tell us one thing after another. Will you not go back, and you will see clearer when you have laid aside fear?

ON THE SAME

If these things are true, and if we are not silly, and are not acting hypocritically when we say that the good of man is in the will, and the evil too, and that everything else does not concern us, why are we still disturbed, why are we still afraid? The things about which we have been busied are in no man's power; and the things which are in the power of others, we care not for. What kind of trouble have we still?

But give me directions. Why should I give you directions? Has not Zeus given you directions? Has he not given to you what is your own free from hindrance and free from impediment, and what is not your own subject to hindrance and impediment? What directions then, what kind of orders did you bring when you came from him? Keep by every means what is your own; do not desire what belongs to others. Fidelity (integrity) is your own, virtuous shame is your own; who then can take these things from you? who else than yourself will hinder you from using them? But how do you act? When you seek what is not your own, you lose that which is your own. Having such promptings and commands from Zeus, what kind do you still ask from me? Am I more powerful than he, am I more worthy of confidence? But if you observe these, do you want any others besides? "Well, but he has not given these orders," you will say. Produce your praecognitions (Greek: *prolaepseis*), produce these proofs of philosophers, produce what you have often heard, and produce what you have said yourself, produce what you have read, produce what you have meditated on; and you will then see that all these things are from God.

If I have set my admiration on the poor body, I have given myself up to be a slave; if on my poor possessions, I also make myself a slave. For I immediately make it plain with what I may be caught; as if the snake draws in his head, I tell you to strike that part of him which he guards; and do you be assured that whatever part you choose to guard, that part your master will attack. Remembering this, whom will you still flatter or fear?

But I should like to sit where the Senators sit. Do you see that you are putting yourself in straits, you are squeezing yourself? How then shall I see well in any other way in the amphitheatre? Man, do not be a spectator at all, and you will not be squeezed. Why do you give yourself trouble? Or wait a little, and when the spectacle is over, seat yourself in the place reserved for the Senators and sun yourself. For remember this general truth, that it is we who squeeze ourselves, who put ourselves in straits; that is, our opinions squeeze us and put us in straits. For what is it to be reviled? Stand by a stone and revile it, and what will you gain? If then a man listens like a stone, what profit is there to the reviler? But if the reviler has as a stepping-stone (or ladder) the weakness of him who is reviled, then he accomplishes something. Strip him. What do you mean by him? Lay hold of his garment, strip it off. I have insulted you. Much good may it do you.

This was the practice of Socrates; this was the reason why he always had one face. But we choose to practise and study anything rather than the means by which we shall be unimpeded and free. You say: "Philosophers talk paradoxes." But are there no paradoxes in the other arts? And what is more paradoxical than to puncture a man's eye in order that he may see? If any one said this to a man ignorant of the surgical art, would he not ridicule the speaker? Where is the wonder, then, if in philosophy also many things which are true appear paradoxical to the inexperienced?

IN HOW MANY WAYS APPEARANCES EXIST, AND WHAT AIDS WE SHOULD PROVIDE AGAINST THEM

Appearances are to us in four ways. For either things appear as they are; or they are not, and do not even appear to be; or they are, and do not appear to be; or they are not, and yet appear to be. Further, in all these cases to form a right judgment (to hit the mark) is the office of an educated man. But whatever it is that annoys (troubles) us, to that we ought to apply a remedy. If the sophisms of Pyrrho and of the Academics are what annoys (troubles), we must apply the remedy to them. If it is the persuasion of appearances, by which some things appear to be good, when they are not good, let us seek a remedy for this. If it is habit which annoys us, we must try to seek aid against habit. What aid, then, can we find against habit? The contrary habit. You hear the ignorant say: "That unfortunate person is dead; his father and mother are overpowered with sorrow; he was cut off by an untimely death and in a foreign land." Hear the contrary way of speaking. Tear yourself from these expressions; oppose to one habit the contrary habit; to sophistry oppose reason, and the exercise and discipline of reason; against persuasive (deceitful) appearances we ought to have manifest praecognitions (Greek: *prolaepseis*), cleared of all impurities and ready to hand.

When death appears an evil, we ought to have this rule in readiness, that it is fit to avoid evil things, and that death is a necessary thing. For what shall I do, and where shall I escape it? Suppose that I am not Sarpedon, the son of Zeus, nor able to speak in this noble way. I will go and I am resolved either to behave bravely myself or to give to another the opportunity of doing so; if I cannot succeed in doing anything myself, I will not grudge another the doing of something noble. Suppose that it is above our power to act thus; is it not in our power to reason thus? Tell me where I can escape death; discover for me the country, show me the men to whom I must go, whom death does not visit. Discover to me a charm against death. If I have not one, what do you wish me to do? I cannot escape from death. Shall I not escape from the fear of death, but shall I die lamenting and trembling? For the origin of perturbation is this, to wish for something, and that this should not happen. Therefore if I am able to change externals according to my wish, I change them; but if I cannot, I am ready to tear out the eyes of him who hinders me. For the nature of man is not to endure to be deprived of the good, and not to endure the falling into the evil. Then at last, when I am neither able to change circumstances nor to tear out the eyes of him who hinders me, I sit down and groan, and abuse whom I can, Zeus and the rest of the gods. For if they do not care for me, what are they to me? Yes, but you will be an impious man. In what respect, then, will it be worse for me than it is now? To sum up, remember that unless piety and your interest be in the same thing, piety cannot be maintained in any man. Do not these things seem necessary (true)?

THAT WE OUGHT NOT TO BE ANGRY WITH MEN; AND WHAT ARE THE SMALL AND THE GREAT THINGS AMONG MEN

What is the cause of assenting to anything? The fact that it appears to be true. It is not possible then to assent to that which appears not to be true. Why? Because this is the nature of the understanding, to incline to the true, to be dissatisfied with the false, and in matters uncertain to withhold assent. What is the proof of this? Imagine (persuade yourself), if you can, that it is now night. It is not possible. Take away your persuasion that it is day. It is not possible. Persuade yourself or take away your persuasion that the stars are even in number. It is impossible. When then any man assents to that which is false, be assured that he did not intend to assent to it as false, for every soul is unwillingly deprived of the truth, as Plato says; but the falsity seemed to him to be true. Well, in acts what have we of the like kind as we have here truth or falsehood? We have the fit and the not fit (duty and not duty), the profitable and the unprofitable, that which is suitable to a person and that which is not, and whatever is like these. Can then a man think that a thing is useful to him and not choose it? He cannot. How says Medea?

"'Tis true I know what evil I shall do,
But passion overpowers the better counsel."

She thought that to indulge her passion and take vengeance on her husband was more profitable than to spare her children. It was so; but she was deceived. Show her plainly that she is deceived, and she will not do it; but so long as you do not show it, what can she follow except that which appears to herself (her opinion)? Nothing else. Why then are you angry with the unhappy woman that she has been bewildered about the most important things, and is become a viper instead of a human creature? And why not, if it is possible, rather pity, as we pity the blind and the lame, so those who are blinded and maimed in the faculties which are supreme?

Whoever then clearly remembers this, that to man the measure of every act is the appearance (the opinion), whether the thing appears good or bad. If good, he is free from blame; if bad, himself suffers the penalty, for it is impossible that he who is deceived can be one person, and he who suffers another person—whoever remembers this will not be angry with any man, will not be vexed at any man, will not revile or blame any man, nor hate, nor quarrel with any man.

Does a man then differ in no respect from a stork? Don't suppose that I say so; but there is no difference in these matters (which I have mentioned). In what then is the difference? Seek and you will find that there is a difference in another matter. See whether it is not in a man the understanding of what he does, see if it is not in social community, in fidelity, in modesty, in steadfastness, in intelligence. Where then is the great good and evil in men? It is where the difference is. If the difference is preserved and remains fenced round, and neither modesty is destroyed, nor fidelity, nor intelligence, then the man also is preserved; but if any of these things is destroyed and stormed like a city, then the man too perishes: and in this consist the great things. Alexander, you say, sustained great damage then when the Hellenes invaded and when they ravaged Troy, and when his brothers perished. By no means; for no man is damaged by an action which is not his own; but what happened at that time was only the destruction of stork's nests. Now the ruin of Alexander was when he lost the character of modesty, fidelity, regard to hospitality, and to decency. When was Achilles ruined? Was it when Patroclus died? Not so. But it happened when he began to be angry, when he wept for a girl, when he forgot that he was at Troy not to get mistresses, but to fight. These things are the ruin of men, this is being besieged, this is the destruction of cities, when right opinions are destroyed, when they are corrupted.

ON CONSTANCY (OR FIRMNESS)

The being (nature) of the good is a certain will; the being of the bad is a certain kind of will. What, then, are externals? Materials for the will, about which the will being conversant shall obtain its own good or evil. How shall it obtain the good? If it does not admire (over-value) the materials; for the opinions about the materials, if the opinions are right, make the will good: but perverse and distorted opinions make the will bad. God has fixed this law, and says, "If you would have anything good, receive it from yourself." You say, No, but I will have it from another. Do not so: but receive it from yourself. Therefore when the tyrant threatens and calls me, I say, Whom do you threaten? If he says, I will put you in chains, I say, You threaten my hands and my feet. If he says, I will cut off your head, I reply, You threaten my head. If he says, I will throw you into prison, I say, You threaten the whole of this poor body. If he threatens me with banishment, I say the same. Does he then not threaten you at all? If I feel that all these things do not concern me, he does not threaten me at all; but if I fear any of them, it is I whom he threatens. Whom then do I fear? the master of what? The master of things which are in my own power? There is no such master. Do I fear the master of things which are not in my power? And what are these things to me?

Do you philosophers then teach us to despise kings? I hope not. Who among us teaches to claim against them the power over things which they possess? Take my poor body, take my property, take my reputation, take those who are about me. If I advise any persons to claim these things, they may truly accuse me. Yes, but I intend to command your opinions also. And who has given you this power? How can you conquer the opinion of another man? By applying terror to it, he replies, I will conquer it. Do you not know that opinion conquers itself, and is not conquered by another? But nothing else can conquer will except the will itself. For this reason too the law of God is most powerful and most just, which is this: Let the stronger always be superior to the weaker. Ten are stronger than one. For what? For putting in chains, for killing, for dragging whither they choose, for taking away what a man has. The ten therefore conquer the one in this in which they are stronger. In what then are the ten weaker? If the one possesses right opinions and the others do not. Well then, can the ten conquer in this matter? How is it possible? If we were placed in the scales, must not the heavier draw down the scale in which it is.

How strange then that Socrates should have been so treated by the Athenians. Slave, why do you say Socrates? Speak of the thing as it is: how strange that the poor body of Socrates should have been carried off and dragged to prison by stronger men, and that anyone should have given hemlock to the poor body of Socrates, and that it should breathe out the life. Do these things seem strange, do they seem unjust, do you on account of these things blame God? Had Socrates then no equivalent for these things? Where then for him was the nature of good? Whom shall we listen to, you or him? And what does Socrates say? "Anytus and Melitus can kill me, but they cannot hurt me." And further, he says, "If it so pleases God, so let it be."

But show me that he who has the inferior principles overpowers him who is superior in principles. You will never show this, nor come near showing it; for this is the law of nature and of God that the superior shall always overpower the inferior. In what? In that in which it is superior. One body is stronger than another: many are stronger than one: the thief is stronger than he who is not a thief. This is the reason why I also lost my lamp, because in wakefulness the thief was superior to me. But the man bought the lamp at this price: for a lamp he became a thief, a faithless fellow, and like a wild beast. This seemed to him a good bargain. Be it so. But a man has seized me by the cloak, and is drawing me to the public place: then others bawl out, Philosopher, what has been the use of your opinions? see, you are dragged to prison, you are going to be beheaded. And what system of philosophy (Greek: *eisagogaen*) could I have made so that, if a stronger man should have laid hold of my cloak, I should not be dragged off; that if ten men should have laid hold of me and cast me into prison, I should not be cast in? Have I learned nothing else then? I have learned to see that everything which happens, if it be independent of my will, is nothing to me. I may ask, if you have not gained by this. Why then do you seek advantage in anything else than in that in which you have learned that advantage is?

Will you not leave the small arguments (Greek: *logaria*) about these matters to others, to lazy fellows, that they may sit in a corner and receive their sorry pay, or grumble that no one gives them anything; and will you not come forward and make use of what you have learned? For it is not these small arguments that are wanted now; the writings of the Stoics are full of them. What then is the thing which is wanted? A man who shall apply them, one who by his acts shall bear testimony to his words. Assume, I intreat you, this character, that we may no longer use in the schools the examples of the ancients, but may have some example of our own.

To whom then does the contemplation of these matters (philosophical inquiries) belong? To him who has leisure, for man is an animal that loves contemplation. But it is shameful to contemplate these things as runaway slaves do; we should sit, as in a theatre, free from distraction, and listen at one time to the tragic actor, at another time to the lute-player; and not do as slaves do. As soon as the slave has taken his station he praises the actor and at the same time looks round; then if any one calls out his master's name, the slave is immediately frightened and disturbed. It is shameful for philosophers thus to contemplate the works of nature. For what is a master? Man is not the master of man; but death is, and life and pleasure and pain; for if he comes without these things, bring Caesar to me and you will see how firm I am. But when he shall come with these things, thundering and lightning, and when I am afraid of them, what do I do then except to recognize my master like the runaway slave? But so long as I have any respite from these terrors, as a runaway slave stands in the theatre, so do I. I bathe, I drink, I sing; but all this I do with terror and uneasiness. But if I shall release myself from my masters, that is from those things by means of which masters are formidable, what further trouble have I, what master have I still?

What then, ought we to publish these things to all men? No, but we ought to accommodate ourselves to the ignorant (Greek: *tois idiotais*) and to say: "This man recommends to me that which he thinks good for himself. I excuse him." For Socrates also excused the jailer who had the charge of him in prison and was weeping when Socrates was going to drink the poison, and said, "How generously he laments over us." Does he then say to the jailer that for this reason we have sent away the women? No, but he says it to his friends who were able to hear (understand) it; and he treats the jailer as a child.

THAT CONFIDENCE (COURAGE) IS NOT INCONSISTENT WITH CAUTION

The opinion of the philosophers perhaps seem to some to be a paradox; but still let us examine as well as we can, if it is true that it is possible to do everything both with caution and with confidence. For caution seems to be in a manner contrary to confidence, and contraries are in no way consistent. That which seems to many to be a paradox in the matter under consideration in my opinion is of this kind; if we asserted that we ought to employ caution and confidence in the same things, men might justly accuse us of bringing together things which cannot be united. But now where is the difficulty in what is said? for if these things are true, which have been often said and often proved, that the nature of good is in the use of appearances, and the nature of evil likewise, and that things independent of our will do not admit either the nature of evil or of good, what paradox do the philosophers assert if they say that where things are not dependent on the will, there you should employ confidence, but where they are dependent on the will, there you should employ caution? For if the bad consists in the bad exercise of the will, caution ought only to be used where things are dependent on the will. But if things independent of the will and not in our power are nothing to us, with respect to these we must employ confidence; and thus we shall both be cautious and confident, and indeed confident because of our caution. For by employing caution towards things which are really bad, it will result that we shall have confidence with respect to things which are not so.

We are then in the condition of deer; when they flee from the huntsmen's feathers in fright, whither do they turn and in what do they seek refuge as safe? They turn to the nets, and thus they perish by confounding things which are objects of fear with things that they ought not to fear. Thus we also act: in what cases do we fear? In things which are independent of the will. In what cases on the contrary do we behave with confidence, as if there were no danger? In things dependent on the will. To be deceived then, or to act rashly, or shamelessly, or with base desire to seek something, does not concern us at all, if we only hit the mark in things which are independent of our will. But where there is death or exile or pain or infamy, there we attempt to run away, there we are struck with terror. Therefore, as we may expect it to happen with those who err in the greatest matters, we convert natural confidence (that is, according to nature) into audacity, desperation, rashness, shamelessness; and we convert natural caution and modesty into cowardice and meanness, which are full of fear and confusion. For if a man should transfer caution to those things in which the will may be exercised and the acts of the will, he will immediately by willing to be cautious have also the power of avoiding what he chooses; but if he transfer it to the things which are not in his power and will, and attempt to avoid the things which are in the power of others, he will of necessity fear, he will be unstable, he will be disturbed; for death or pain is not formidable, but the fear of pain or death. For this reason we commend the poet, who said:

"Not death is evil, but a shameful death."

Confidence (courage) then ought to be employed against death, and caution against the fear of death. But now we do the contrary, and employ against death the attempt to escape; and to our opinion about it we employ carelessness, rashness, and indifference. These things Socrates properly used to call tragic masks; for as to children masks appear terrible and fearful from inexperience, we also are affected in like manner by events (the things which happen in life) for no other reason than children are by masks. For what is a child? Ignorance. What is a child? Want of knowledge. For when a child knows these things, he is in no way inferior to us. What is death? A tragic mask. Turn it and examine it. See, it does not bite. The poor body must be separated from the spirit either now or later as it was separated from it before. Why then are you troubled if it be separated now? for if it is not separated now, it will be separated afterwards. Why? That the period of the universe may be completed, for it has need of the present, and of the future, and of the past. What is pain? A mask. Turn it and examine it. The poor flesh is moved roughly, then on the contrary smoothly. If this does not satisfy (please) you, the door is open; if it does, bear (with things). For the door ought to be open for all occasions; and so we have no trouble.

What then is the fruit of these opinions? It is that which ought to be the most noble and the most becoming to those who are really educated, release from perturbation, release from fear. Freedom. For in these matters we must not believe the many, who say that free persons only ought to be educated, but we should rather believe the philosophers who say that the educated only are free. How is this? In this manner: Is freedom anything else than the power of living as we choose? Nothing else. Tell me then, ye men, do you wish to live in error? We do not. No one then who lives in error is free. Do you wish to live in fear? Do you wish to live in sorrow? Do you wish to live in perturbation? By no means. No one then who is in a state of fear or sorrow or perturbation is free; but whoever is delivered from sorrows and fears and perturbations, he is at the same time also delivered from servitude. How then can we continue to believe you, most dear legislators, when you say, We only allow free persons to be educated? For philosophers say we allow none to be free except the educated; that is, God does not allow it. When then a man has turned round before the praetor his own slave, has he done nothing? He has done something. What? He has turned round his own slave before the praetor. Has he done nothing more? Yes: he is also bound to pay for him the tax called the twentieth. Well then, is not the man who has gone through this ceremony become free? No more than he is become free from perturbations. Have you who are able to turn round (free) others no master? is not money your master, or a girl or a boy, or some tyrant or some friend of the tyrant? Why do you trouble then when you are going off to any trial (danger) of this kind? It is for this reason that I often say, study and hold in readiness these principles by which you may determine what those things are with reference to which you ought to be cautious, courageous in that which does not depend on your will, cautious in that which does depend on it.

OF TRANQUILLITY (FREEDOM FROM PERTURBATION)

Consider, you who are going into court, what you wish to maintain and what you wish to succeed in. For if you wish to maintain a will conformable to nature, you have every security, every facility, you have no troubles. For if you wish to maintain what is in your own power and is naturally free, and if you are content with these, what else do you care for? For who is the master of such things? Who can take them away? If you choose to be modest and faithful, who shall not allow you to be so? If you choose not to be restrained or compelled, who shall compel you to desire what you think that you ought not to desire? who shall compel you to avoid what you do not think fit to avoid? But what do you say? The judge will determine against you something that appears formidable; but that you should also suffer in trying to avoid it, how can he do that? When then the pursuit of objects and the avoiding of them are in your power, what else do you care for? Let this be your preface, this your narrative, this your confirmation, this your victory, this your peroration, this your applause (or the approbation which you will receive).

Therefore Socrates said to one who was reminding him to prepare for his trial, Do you not think then that I have been preparing for it all my life? By what kind of preparation? I have maintained that which was in my own power. How then? I have never done anything unjust either in my private or in my public life.

But if you wish to maintain externals also, your poor body, your little property, and your little estimation, I advise you to make from this moment all possible preparation, and then consider both the nature of your judge and your adversary. If it is necessary to embrace his knees, embrace his knees; if to weep, weep; if to groan, groan. For when you have subjected to externals what is your own, then be a slave and do not resist, and do not sometimes choose to be a slave, and sometimes not choose, but with all your mind be one or the other, either free or a slave, either instructed or uninstructed, either a well-bred cock or a mean one, either endure to be beaten until you die or yield at once; and let it not happen to you to receive many stripes and then to yield. But if these things are base, determine immediately. Where is the nature of evil and good? It is where truth is: where truth is and where nature is, there is caution: where truth is, there is courage where nature is.

For this reason also it is ridiculous to say, Suggest something to me (tell me what to do). What should I suggest to you? Well, form my mind so as to accommodate itself to any event. Why that is just the same as if a man who is ignorant of letters should say, Tell me what to write when any name is proposed to me. For if I should tell him to write Dion, and then another should come and propose to him not the name of Dion but that of Theon, what will be done? what will he write? But if you have practised writing, you are also prepared to write (or to do) anything that is required. If you are not, what can I now suggest? For if circumstances require something else, what will you say, or what will you do? Remember then this general precept and you will need no suggestion. But if you gape after externals, you must of necessity ramble up and down in obedience to the will of your master. And who is the master? He who has the power over the things which you seek to gain or try to avoid.

HOW MAGNANIMITY IS CONSISTENT WITH CARE

Things themselves (materials) are indifferent; but the use of them is not indifferent. How then shall a man preserve firmness and tranquillity, and at the same time be careful and neither rash nor negligent? If he imitates those who play at dice. The counters are indifferent; the dice are indifferent. How do I know what the cast will be? But to use carefully and dexterously the cast of the dice, this is my business. Thus then in life also the chief business is this: distinguish and separate things, and say: Externals are not in my power: will is in my power. Where shall I seek the good and the bad? Within, in the things which are my own. But in what does not belong to you call nothing either good or bad, or profit or damage or anything of the kind.

What then? Should we use such things carelessly? In no way: for this on the other hand is bad for the faculty of the will, and consequently against nature; but we should act carefully because the use is not indifferent, and we should also act with firmness and freedom from perturbations because the material is indifferent. For where the material is not indifferent, there no man can hinder me or compel me. Where I can be hindered and compelled, the obtaining of those things is not in my power, nor is it good or bad; but the use is either bad or good, and the use is in my power. But it is difficult to mingle and to bring together these two things—the carefulness of him who is affected by the matter (or things about him), and the firmness of him who has no regard for it; but it is not impossible: and if it is, happiness is impossible. But we should act as we do in the case of a voyage. What can I do? I can choose the master of the ship, the sailors, the day, the opportunity. Then comes a storm. What more have I to care for? for my part is done. The business belongs to another, the master. But the ship is sinking—what then have I to do? I do the only thing that I can, not to be drowned full of fear, nor screaming nor blaming God, but knowing that what has been produced must also perish: for I am not an immortal being, but a man, a part of the whole, as an hour is a part of the day: I must be present like the hour, and past like the hour. What difference then does it make to me how I pass away, whether by being suffocated or by a fever, for I must pass through some such means.

How then is it said that some external things are according to nature and others contrary to nature? It is said as it might be said if we were separated from union (or society): for to the foot I shall say that it is according to nature for it to be clean; but if you take it as a foot and as a thing not detached (independent), it will befit it both to step into the mud and tread on thorns, and sometimes to be cut off for the good of the whole body; otherwise it is no longer a foot. We should think in some such way about ourselves also. What are you? A man. If you consider yourself as detached from other men, it is according to nature to live to old age, to be rich, to be healthy. But if you consider yourself as a man and a part of a certain whole, it is for the sake of that whole that at one time you should be sick, at another time take a voyage and run into danger, and at another time be in want, and in some cases die prematurely. Why then are you troubled? Do you not know, that as a foot is no longer a foot if it is detached from the body, so you are no longer a man if you are separated from other men. For what is a man? A part of a state, of that first which consists of gods and of men; then of that which is called next to it, which is a small image of the universal state. What then must I be brought to trial; must another have a fever, another sail on the sea, another die, and another be condemned? Yes, for it is impossible in such a universe of things, among so many living together, that such things should not happen, some to one and others to others. It is your duty then since you are come here, to say what you ought, to arrange these things as it is fit. Then some one says, "I shall charge you with doing me wrong." Much good may it do you: I have done my part; but whether you also have done yours, you must look to that; for there is some danger of this too, that it may escape your notice.

OF INDIFFERENCE

The hypothetical proposition is indifferent: the judgment about it is not indifferent, but it is either knowledge or opinion or error. Thus life is indifferent: the use is not indifferent. When any man then tells you that these things also are indifferent, do not become negligent; and when a man invites you to be careful (about such things), do not become abject and struck with admiration of material things. And it is good for you to know your own preparation and power, that in those matters where you have not been prepared, you may keep quiet, and not be vexed, if others have the advantage over you. For you too in syllogisms will claim to have the advantage over them; and if others should be vexed at this, you will console them by saying, "I have learned them, and you have not." Thus also where there is need of any practice, seek not that which is acquired from the need (of such practice), but yield in that matter to those who have had practice, and be yourself content with firmness of mind.

Go and salute a certain person. How? Not meanly. But I have been shut out, for I have not learned to make my way through the window; and when I have found the door shut, I must either come back or enter through the window. But still speak to him.

In what way? Not meanly. But suppose that you have not got what you wanted. Was this your business, and not his? Why then do you claim that which belongs to another? Always remember what is your own, and what belongs to another; and you will not be disturbed. Chrysippus therefore said well, So long as future things are uncertain, I always cling to those which are more adapted to the conservation of that which is according to nature; for God himself has given me the faculty of such choice. But if I knew that it was fated (in the order of things) for me to be sick, I would even move towards it; for the foot also, if it had intelligence, would move to go into the mud. For why are ears of corn produced? Is it not that they may become dry? And do they not become dry that they may be reaped? for they are not separated from communion with other things. If then they had perception, ought they to wish never to be reaped? But this is a curse upon ears of corn to be never reaped. So we must know that in the case of men too it is a curse not to die, just the same as not to be ripened and not to be reaped. But since we must be reaped, and we also know that we are reaped, we are vexed at it; for we neither know what we are nor have we studied what belongs to man, as those who have studied horses know what belongs to horses. But Chrysantas when he was going to strike the enemy checked himself when he heard the trumpet sounding a retreat: so it seemed better to him to obey the general's command than to follow his own inclination. But not one of us chooses, even when necessity summons, readily to obey it, but weeping and groaning we suffer what we do suffer, and we call them "circumstances." What kind of circumstances, man? If you give the name of circumstances to the things which are around you, all things are circumstances; but if you call hardships by this name, what hardship is there in the dying of that which has been produced? But that which destroys is either a sword, or a wheel, or the sea, or a tile, or a tyrant. Why do you care about the way of going down to Hades? All ways are equal. But if you will listen to the truth, the way which the tyrant sends you is shorter. A tyrant never killed a man in six months: but a fever is often a year about it. All these things are only sound and the noise of empty names.

HOW WE OUGHT TO USE DIVINATION

Through an unreasonable regard to divination many of us omit many duties. For what more can the diviner see than death or danger or disease, or generally things of that kind? If then I must expose myself to danger for a friend, and if it is my duty even to die for him, what need have I then for divination? Have I not within me a diviner who has told me the nature of good and of evil, and has explained to me the signs (or marks) of both? What need have I then to consult the viscera of victims or the flight of birds, and why do I submit when he says, It is for your interest? For does he know what is for my interest, does he know what is good; and as he has learned the signs of the viscera, has he also learned the signs of good and evil? For if he knows the signs of these, he knows the signs both of the beautiful and of the ugly, and of the just and of the unjust. Do you tell me, man, what is the thing which is signified for me: is it life or death, poverty or wealth? But whether these things are for my interest or whether they are not, I do not intend to ask you. Why don't you give your opinion on matters of grammar, and why do you give it here about things on which we are all in error and disputing with one another?

What then leads us to frequent use of divination? Cowardice, the dread of what will happen. This is the reason why we flatter the diviners. Pray, master, shall I succeed to the property of my father? Let us see: let us sacrifice on the occasion. Yes, master, as fortune chooses. When he has said, You shall succeed to the inheritance, we thank him as if we received the inheritance from him. The consequence is that they play upon us.

Will you not then seek the nature of good in the rational animal? for if it is not there, you will not choose to say that it exists in any other thing (plant or animal). What then? are not plants and animals also the works of God? They are; but they are not superior things, nor yet parts of the gods. But you are a superior thing; you are a portion separated from the Deity; you have in yourself a certain portion of him. Why then are you ignorant of your own noble descent? Why do you not know whence you came? will you not remember when you are eating who you are who eat and whom you feed? When you are in social intercourse, when you are exercising yourself, when you are engaged in discussion, know you not that you are nourishing a god, that you are exercising a god? Wretch, you are carrying about a god with you, and you know it not. Do you think that I mean some god of silver or of gold, and external? You carry him within yourself, and you perceive not that you are polluting him by impure thoughts and dirty deeds. And if an image of God were present, you would not dare to do any of the things which you are doing; but when God himself is present within and sees all and hears all, you are not ashamed of thinking such things and doing such things, ignorant as you are of your own nature and subject to the anger of God. Then why do we fear when we are sending a young man from the school into active life, lest he should do anything improperly, eat improperly, have improper intercourse with women; and lest the rags in which he is wrapped should debase him, lest fine garments should make him proud. This youth (if he acts thus) does not know his own

God; he knows not with whom he sets out (into the world). But can we endure when he says, "I wish I had you (God) with me." Have you not God with you? and do you seek for any other when you have him? or will God tell you anything else than this? If you were a statue of Phidias, either Athena or Zeus, you would think both of yourself and of the artist, and if you had any understanding (power of perception) you would try to do nothing unworthy of him who made you or of yourself, and try not to appear in an unbecoming dress (attitude) to those who look upon you. But now because Zeus has made you, for this reason do you care not how you shall appear? And yet is the artist (in the one case) like the artist in the other? or the work in the one case like the other? And what work of an artist, for instance, has in itself the faculties, which the artist shows in making it? Is it not marble or bronze, or gold or ivory? and the Athena of Phidias, when she has once extended the hand and received in it the figure of Victory, stands in that attitude for ever. But the works of God have power of motion, they breathe, they have the faculty of using the appearances of things and the power of examining them. Being the work of such an artist do you dishonor him? And what shall I say, not only that he made you, but also entrusted you to yourself and made you a deposit to yourself? Will you not think of this too, but do you also dishonor your guardianship? But if God had entrusted an orphan to you, would you thus neglect him? He has delivered yourself to your own care, and says: "I had no one fitter to entrust him to than yourself; keep him for me such as he is by nature, modest, faithful, erect, unterrified, free from passion and perturbation." And then you do not keep him such.

But some will say, Whence has this fellow got the arrogance which he displays and these supercilious looks? I have not yet so much gravity as befits a philosopher; for I do not yet feel confidence in what I have learned and in what I have assented to. I still fear my own weakness. Let me get confidence and then you shall see a countenance such as I ought to have and an attitude such as I ought to have; then I will show to you the statue, when it is perfected, when it is polished. What do you expect? a supercilious countenance? Does the Zeus at Olympia lift up his brow? No, his look is fixed as becomes him who is ready to say:

> Irrevocable is my word and shall not fail.—*Iliad*, i., 526.

Such will I show myself to you, faithful, modest, noble, free from perturbation. What, and immortal, too, except from old age, and from sickness? No, but dying as becomes a god, sickening as becomes a god. This power I possess; this I can do. But the rest I do not possess, nor can I do. I will show the nerves (strength) of a philosopher. What nerves are these? A desire never disappointed, an aversion which never falls on that which it would avoid, a proper pursuit (Greek: *hormaen*), a diligent purpose, an assent which is not rash. These you shall see.

THAT WHEN WE CANNOT FULFIL THAT WHICH THE CHARACTER OF A MAN PROMISES, WE ASSUME THE CHARACTER OF A PHILOSOPHER

It is no common (easy) thing to do this only, to fulfil the promise of a man's nature. For what is a man? The answer is, A rational and mortal being. Then by the rational faculty from whom are we separated? From wild beasts. And from what others? From sheep and like animals. Take care then to do nothing like a wild beast; but if you do, you have lost the character of a man; you have not fulfilled your promise. See that you do nothing like a sheep; but if you do, in this case also the man is lost. What then do we do as sheep? When we act gluttonously, when we act lewdly, when we act rashly, filthily, inconsiderately, to what have we declined? To sheep. What have we lost? The rational faculty. When we act contentiously and harmfully and passionately and violently, to what have we declined? To wild beasts. Consequently some of us are great wild beasts, and others little beasts, of a bad disposition and small, whence we may say, Let me be eaten by a lion. But in all these ways the promise of a man acting as a man is destroyed. For when is a conjunctive (complex) proposition maintained? When it fulfils what its nature promises; so that the preservation of a complex proposition is when it is a conjunction of truths. When is a disjunctive maintained? When it fulfils what it promises. When are flutes, a lyre, a horse, a dog, preserved? (When they severally keep their promise.) What is the wonder then if man also in like manner is preserved, and in like manner is lost? Each man is improved and preserved by corresponding acts, the carpenter by acts of carpentry, the grammarian by acts of grammar. But if a man accustoms himself to write ungrammatically, of necessity his art will be corrupted and destroyed. Thus modest actions preserve the modest man, and immodest actions destroy him; and actions of fidelity preserve the faithful man, and the contrary actions destroy him. And on the other hand contrary actions strengthen contrary characters: shamelessness strengthens the shameless man, faithlessness the faithless man, abusive words the abusive man, anger the man of an angry temper, and unequal receiving and giving make the avaricious man more avaricious.

For this reason philosophers admonish us not to be satisfied with learning only, but also to add study, and then practice. For we have long been accustomed to do contrary things, and we put in practice opinions which are contrary to true opinions. If then we shall not also put in practice right opinions, we shall be nothing more than the expositors of the opinions of others. For now who among us is not able to discourse according to the rules of art about good and evil things (in this fashion)? That of things some are good, and some are bad, and some are indifferent: the good then are virtues, and the things which participate in virtues; and the bad are the contrary; and the indifferent are wealth, health, reputation. Then, if in the midst of our talk there should happen some greater noise than usual, or some of those who are present should laugh at us, we are disturbed. Philosopher, where are the things which you were talking about? Whence did you produce and utter them? From the lips, and thence only. Why then do you corrupt the aids provided by others? Why do you treat the weightiest matters as if you were playing a game of dice? For it is one thing to lay up bread and wine as in a storehouse, and another thing to eat. That which has been eaten, is digested, distributed, and is become sinews, flesh, bones, blood, healthy color, healthy breath. Whatever is stored up, when you choose you can readily take and show it; but you have no other advantage from it except so far as to appear to possess it. For what is the difference between explaining these doctrines and those of men who have different opinions? Sit down now and explain according to the rules of art the opinions of Epicurus, and perhaps you will explain his opinions in a more useful manner than Epicurus himself. Why then do you call yourself a Stoic? Why do you deceive the many? Why do you act the part of a Jew, when you are a Greek? Do you not see how (why) each is called a Jew, or a Syrian, or an Egyptian? and when we see a man inclining to two sides, we are accustomed to say, This man is not a Jew, but he acts as one. But when he has assumed the affects of one who has been imbued with Jewish doctrine and has adopted that sect, then he is in fact and he is named a Jew.

HOW WE MAY DISCOVER THE DUTIES OF LIFE FROM NAMES

Consider who you are. In the first place, you are a man; and this is one who has nothing superior to the faculty of the will, but all other things subjected to it; and the faculty itself he possesses unenslaved and free from subjection. Consider then from what things you have been separated by reason. You have been separated from wild beasts; you have been separated from domestic animals (Greek: *probaton*). Further, you are a citizen of the world, and a part of it, not one of the subservient (serving), but one of the principal (ruling) parts, for you are capable of comprehending the divine administration and of considering the connection of things. What then does the character of a citizen promise (profess)? To hold nothing as profitable to himself; to deliberate about nothing as if he were detached from the community, but to act as the hand or foot would do, if they had reason and understood the constitution of nature, for they would never put themselves in motion nor desire anything otherwise than with reference to the whole. Therefore, the philosophers say well, that if the good man had foreknowledge of what would happen, he would cooperate towards his own sickness and death and mutilation, since he knows that these things are assigned to him according to the universal arrangement, and that the whole is superior to the part, and the state to the citizen. But now because we do not know the future, it is our duty to stick to the things which are in their nature more suitable for our choice, for we were made among other things for this.

After this, remember that you are a son. What does this character promise? To consider that everything which is the son's belongs to the father, to obey him in all things, never to blame him to another, nor to say or do anything which does him injury, to yield to him in all things and give way, co-operating with him as far as you can. After this know that you are a brother also, and that to this character it is due to make concessions; to be easily persuaded, to speak good of your brother, never to claim in opposition to him any of the things which are independent of the will, but readily to give them up, that you may have the larger share in what is dependent on the will. For see what a thing it is, in place of a lettuce, if it should so happen, or a seat, to gain for yourself goodness of disposition. How great is the advantage.

Next to this, if you are a senator of any state, remember that you are a senator; if a youth, that you are a youth; if an old man, that you are an old man; for each of such names, if it comes to be examined, marks out the proper duties. But if you go and blame your brother, I say to you, You have forgotten who you are and what is your name. In the next place, if you were a smith and made a wrong use of the hammer, you would have forgotten the smith; and if you have forgotten the brother and instead of a brother have become an enemy, would you appear not to have changed one thing for another in that case? And if instead of a man, who is a tame animal and social, you are become a mischievous wild beast, treacherous, and biting, have you lost nothing? But (I suppose) you must lose a bit of money that you may suffer damage? And does the loss of nothing else do a man damage? If you had lost the art of grammar or music, would you think the loss of it a damage? and if you shall lose modesty, moderation (*Greek: chtastolaen*) and gentleness, do you think the loss nothing? And yet the things first mentioned are lost by some cause external and independent of the will, and the second by our own fault; and as to the first neither to have them nor to lose them is shameful; but as to the second, not to have them and to lose them is shameful and matter of reproach and a misfortune.

What then? shall I not hurt him who has hurt me? In the first place consider what hurt (Greek: *blabae*) is, and remember what you have heard from the philosophers. For if the good consists in the will (purpose, intention, Greek: *proaireeis*), and the evil also in the will, see if what you say is not this: What then, since that man has hurt himself by doing an unjust act to me, shall I not hurt myself by doing some unjust act to him? Why do we not imagine to ourselves (mentally think of) something of this kind? But where there is any detriment to the body or to our possession, there is harm there; and where the same thing happens to the faculty of the will, there is (you suppose) no harm; for he who has been deceived or he who has done an unjust act neither suffers in the head nor in the eye nor in the hip, nor does he lose his estate; and we wish for nothing else than (security to) these things. But whether we shall have the will modest and faithful or shameless and faithless, we care not the least, except only in the school so far as a few words are concerned. Therefore our proficiency is limited to these few words; but beyond them it does not exist even in the slightest degree.

WHAT THE BEGINNING OF PHILOSOPHY IS

The beginning of philosophy, to him at least who enters on it in the right way and by the door is a consciousness of his own weakness and inability about necessary things; for we come into the world with no natural notion of a right-angled triangle, or of a diesis (a quarter tone), or of a half-tone; but we learn each of these things by a certain transmission according to art; and for this reason those who do not know them do not think that they know them. But as to good and evil, and beautiful and ugly, and becoming and unbecoming, and happiness and misfortune, and proper and improper, and what we ought to do and what we ought not to do, who ever came into the world without having an innate idea of them? Wherefore we all use these names, and we endeavor to fit the preconceptions to the several cases (things) thus: he has done well; he has not done well; he has done as he ought, not as he ought; he has been unfortunate, he has been fortunate; he is unjust, he is just; who does not use these names? who among us defers the use of them till he has learned them, as he defers the use of the words about lines (geometrical figures) or sounds? And the cause of this is that we come into the world already taught as it were by nature some things on this matter (Greek: *topon*), and proceeding from these we have added to them self-conceit (Greek: *oiaesin*). For why, a man says, do I not know the beautiful and the ugly? Have I not the notion of it? You have. Do I not adapt it to particulars? You do. Do I not then adapt it properly? In that lies the whole question; and conceit is added here; for beginning from these things which are admitted men proceed to that which is matter of dispute by means of unsuitable adaptation; for if they possessed this power of adaptation in addition to those things, what would hinder them from being perfect? But now since you think that you properly adapt the preconceptions to the particulars, tell me whence you derive this (assume that you do so). Because I think so. But it does not seem so to another, and he thinks that he also makes a proper adaptation; or does he not think so? He does think so. Is it possible then that both of you can properly apply the preconceptions to things about which you have contrary opinions? It is not possible. Can you then show us anything better towards adapting the preconceptions beyond your thinking that you do? Does the madman do any other things than the things which seem to him right? Is then this criterion sufficient for him also? It is not sufficient. Come then to something which is superior to seeming (Greek: *tou dochein*). What is this?

Observe, this is the beginning of philosophy, a perception of the disagreement of men with one another, and an inquiry into the cause of the disagreement, and a condemnation and distrust of that which only "seems," and a certain investigation of that which "seems" whether it "seems" rightly, and a discovery of some rule (Greek: *chanonos*), as we have discovered a balance in the determination of weights, and a carpenter's rule (or square) in the case of straight and crooked things.—This is the beginning of philosophy. Must we say that all things are right which seem so to all? And how is it possible that contradictions can be right?—Not all then, but all which seem to us to be right.—How more to you than those which seem right to the Syrians? why more than what seem right to the Egyptians? why more than what seems right to me or to any other man? Not at all more. What then "seems" to every man is not sufficient for determining what "is"; for neither in the case of weights nor measures are we satisfied with the bare appearance, but in each case we have discovered a certain rule. In this matter then is there no rule superior to what "seems"? And how is it possible that the most necessary things among men should have no sign (mark), and be incapable of being discovered? There is then some rule. And why then do we not seek the rule and discover it, and afterwards use it without varying from it, not even stretching out the finger without it? For this, I think, is that which when it is discovered cures of their madness those who use mere "seeming" as a measure, and misuse it; so that for the future proceeding from certain things (principles) known and made clear we may use in the case of particular things the preconceptions which are distinctly fixed.

What is the matter presented to us about which we are inquiring? Pleasure (for example). Subject it to the rule, throw it into the balance. Ought the good to be such a thing that it is fit that we have confidence in it? Yes. And in which we ought to confide? It ought to be. Is it fit to trust to anything which is insecure? No. Is then pleasure anything secure? No. Take it then and throw it out of the scale, and drive it far away from the place of good things. But if you are not sharp-sighted, and one balance is not enough for you, bring another. Is it fit to be elated over what is good? Yes. Is it proper then to be elated over present pleasure? See that you do not say that it is proper; but if you do, I shall then not think you worthy even of the balance. Thus things are tested and weighed when the rules are ready. And to philosophize is this, to examine and confirm the rules; and then to use them when they are known is the act of a wise and good man.

OF DISPUTATION OR DISCUSSION

What things a man must learn in order to be able to apply the art of disputation, has been accurately shown by our philosophers (the Stoics); but with respect to the proper use of the things, we are entirely without practice. Only give to any of us, whom you please, an illiterate man to discuss with, and he cannot discover how to deal with the man. But when he has moved the man a little, if he answers beside the purpose, he does not know how to treat him, but he then either abuses or ridicules him, and says, He is an illiterate man; it is not possible to do anything with him. Now a guide, when he has found a man out of the road, leads him into the right way; he does not ridicule or abuse him and then leave him. Do you also show the illiterate man the truth, and you will see that he follows. But so long as you do not show him the truth, do not ridicule him, but rather feel your own incapacity.

Now this was the first and chief peculiarity of Socrates, never to be irritated in argument, never to utter anything abusive, anything insulting, but to bear with abusive persons and to put an end to the quarrel. If you would know what great power he had in this way, read the Symposium of Xenophon, and you will see how many quarrels he put an end to. Hence with good reason in the poets also this power is most highly praised:

> Quickly with skill he settles great disputes.
> Hesiod, *Theogony*, v. 87.

ON ANXIETY (SOLICITUDE)

When I see a man anxious, I say, What does this man want? If he did not want something which is not in his power, how could he be anxious? For this reason a lute player when he is singing by himself has no anxiety, but when he enters the theatre, he is anxious, even if he has a good voice and plays well on the lute; for he not only wishes to sing well, but also to obtain applause: but this is not in his power. Accordingly, where he has skill, there he has confidence. Bring any single person who knows nothing of music, and the musician does not care for him. But in the matter where a man knows nothing and has not been practised, there he is anxious. What matter is this? He knows not what a crowd is or what the praise of a crowd is. However, he has learned to strike the lowest chord and the highest; but what the praise of the many is, and what power it has in life, he neither knows nor has he thought about it. Hence he must of necessity tremble and grow pale. Is any man then afraid about things which are not evils? No. Is he afraid about things which are evils, but still so far within his power that they may not happen? Certainly he is not. If then the things which are independent of the will are neither good nor bad, and all things which do depend on the will are within our power, and no man can either take them from us or give them to us, if we do not choose, where is room left for anxiety? But we are anxious about our poor body, our little property, about the will of Caesar; but not anxious about things internal. Are we anxious about not forming a false opinion? No, for this is in my power. About not exerting our movements contrary to nature? No, not even about this. When then you see a man pale, as the physician says, judging from the complexion, this man's spleen is disordered, that man's liver; so also say, this man's desire and aversion are disordered, he is not in the right way, he is in a fever. For nothing else changes the color, or causes trembling or chattering of the teeth, or causes a man to

Sink in his knees and shift from foot to foot.
Iliad, xiii., 281.

For this reason, when Zeno was going to meet Antigonus, he was not anxious, for Antigonus had no power over any of the things which Zeno admired; and Zeno did not care for those things over which Antigonus had power. But Antigonus was anxious when he was going to meet Zeno, for he wished to please Zeno; but this was a thing external (out of his power). But Zeno did not want to please Antigonus; for no man who is skilled in any art wishes to please one who has no such skill.

Should I try to please you? Why? I suppose, you know the measure by which one man is estimated by another. Have you taken pains to learn what is a good man and what is a bad man, and how a man becomes one or the other? Why then are you not good yourself? How, he replies, am I not good? Because no good man laments or groans or weeps, no good man is pale and trembles, or says, How will he receive me, how will he listen to me? Slave, just as it pleases him. Why do you care about what belongs to others? Is it now his fault if he receives badly what proceeds from you? Certainly. And is it possible that a fault should be one man's, and the evil in another? No. Why then are you anxious about that which belongs to others?

Your question is reasonable; but I am anxious how I shall speak to him. Cannot you then speak to him as you choose? But I fear that I may be disconcerted? If you are going to write the name of Dion, are you afraid that you would be disconcerted? By no means. Why? is it not because you have practised writing the name? Certainly. Well, if you were going to read the name, would you not feel the same? and why? Because every art has a certain strength and confidence in the things which belong to it. Have you then not practised speaking? and what else did you learn in the school? Syllogisms and sophistical propositions? For what purpose? was it not for the purpose of discoursing skilfully? and is not discoursing skilfully the same as discoursing seasonably and cautiously and with intelligence, and also without making mistakes and without hindrance, and besides all this with confidence? Yes. When then you are mounted on a horse and go into a plain, are you anxious at being matched against a man who is on foot, and anxious in a matter in which you are practised, and he is not? Yes, but that person (to whom I am going to speak) has power to kill me. Speak the truth, then, unhappy man, and do not brag, nor claim to be a philosopher, nor refuse to acknowledge your masters, but so long as you present this handle in your body, follow every man who is stronger than yourself. Socrates used to practice speaking, he who talked as he did to the tyrants, to the dicasts (judges), he who talked in his prison. Diogenes had practised speaking, he who spoke as he did to Alexander, to the pirates, to the person who bought him. These men were confident in the things which they practised. But do you walk off to your own affairs and never leave them: go and sit in a corner, and weave syllogisms, and propose them to another. There is not in you the man who can rule a state.

TO NASO

When a certain Roman entered with his son and listened to one reading, Epictetus said, This is the method of instruction; and he stopped. When the Roman asked him to go on, Epictetus said, Every art when it is taught causes labor to him who is unacquainted with it and is unskilled in it, and indeed the things which proceed from the arts immediately show their use in the purpose for which they were made; and most of them contain something attractive and pleasing. For indeed to be present and to observe how a shoemaker learns is not a pleasant thing; but the shoe is useful and also not disagreeable to look at. And the discipline of a smith when he is learning is very disagreeable to one who chances to be present and is a stranger to the art: but the work shows the use of the art. But you will see this much more in music; for if you are present while a person is learning, the discipline will appear most disagreeable; and yet the results of music are pleasing and delightful to those who know nothing of music. And here we conceive the work of a philosopher to be something of this kind: he must adapt his wish (Greek: *boulaesin*) to what is going on, so that neither any of the things which are taking place shall take place contrary to our wish, nor any of the things which do not take place shall not take place when we wish that they should. From this the result is to those who have so arranged the work of philosophy, not to fail in the desire, nor to fall in with that which they would avoid; without uneasiness, without fear, without perturbation to pass through life themselves, together with their associates maintaining the relations both natural and acquired, as the relation of son, of father, of brother, of citizen, of man, of wife, of neighbor, of fellow-traveller, of ruler, of ruled. The work of a philosopher we conceive to be something like this. It remains next to inquire how this must be accomplished.

We see then that the carpenter (Greek: *techton*) when he has learned certain things becomes a carpenter; the pilot by learning certain things becomes a pilot. May it not then in philosophy also not be sufficient to wish to be wise and good, and that there is also a necessity to learn certain things? We inquire then what these things are. The philosophers say that we ought first to learn that there is a God and that he provides for all things; also that it is not possible to conceal from him our acts, or even our intentions and thoughts. The next thing is to learn what is the nature of the gods; for such as they are discovered to be, he, who would please and obey them, must try with all his power to be like them. If the divine is faithful, man also must be faithful; if it is free, man also must be free; if beneficent, man also must be beneficent; if magnanimous, man also must be magnanimous; as being then an imitator of God he must do and say everything consistently with this fact.

TO OR AGAINST THOSE WHO OBSTINATELY PERSIST IN WHAT THEY HAVE DETERMINED

When some persons have heard these words, that a man ought to be constant (firm), and that the will is naturally free and not subject to compulsion, but that all other things are subject to hindrance, to slavery, and are in the power of others, they suppose that they ought without deviation to abide by everything which they have determined. But in the first place that which has been determined ought to be sound (true). I require tone (sinews) in the body, but such as exists in a healthy body, in an athletic body; but if it is plain to me that you have the tone of a frenzied man and you boast of it, I shall say to you, Man, seek the physician; this is not tone, but atony (deficiency in right tone). In a different way something of the same kind is felt by those who listen to these discourses in a wrong manner; which was the case with one of my companions, who for no reason resolved to starve himself to death. I heard of it when it was the third day of his abstinence from food, and I went to inquire what had happened. "I have resolved," he said. "But still tell me what it was which induced you to resolve; for if you have resolved rightly, we shall sit with you and assist you to depart, but if you have made an unreasonable resolution, change your mind." "We ought to keep to our determinations." "What are you doing, man? We ought to keep not to all our determinations, but to those which are right; for if you are now persuaded that it is right, do not change your mind, if you think fit, but persist and say, We ought to abide by our determinations. Will you not make the beginning and lay the foundation in an inquiry whether the determination is sound or not sound, and so then build on it firmness and security? But if you lay a rotten and ruinous foundation, will not your miserable little building fall down the sooner, the more and the stronger are the materials which you shall lay on it? Without any reason would you withdraw from us out of life a man who is a friend and a companion, a citizen of the same city, both the great and the small city? Then while you are committing murder and destroying a man who has done no wrong, do you say that you ought to abide by your determinations? And if it ever in any way came into your head to kill me, ought you to abide by your determinations?"

Now this man was with difficulty persuaded to change his mind. But it is impossible to convince some persons at present; so that I seem now to know what I did not know before, the meaning of the common saying, that you can neither persuade nor break a fool. May it never be my lot to have a wise fool for my friend; nothing is more untractable. "I am determined," the man says. Madmen are also, but the more firmly they form a judgment on things which do not exist, the more hellebore they require. Will you not act like a sick man and call in the physician?—I am sick, master, help me; consider what I must do: it is my duty to obey you. So it is here also: I know not what I ought to do, but I am come to learn.—Not so; but speak to me about other things: upon this I have determined.—What other things? for what is greater and more useful than for you to be persuaded that it is not sufficient to have made your determination and not to change it. This is the tone (energy) of madness, not of health.—I will die, if you compel me to this.—Why, man? What has happened?—I have determined—I have had a lucky escape that you have not determined to kill me—I take no money. Why?—I have determined—Be assured that with the very tone (energy) which you now use in refusing to take, there is nothing to hinder you at some time from inclining without reason to take money, and then saying, I have determined. As in a distempered body, subject to defluxions, the humor inclines sometimes to these parts, and then to those, so too a sickly soul knows not which way to incline; but if to this inclination and movement there is added a tone (obstinate resolution), then the evil becomes past help and cure.

THAT WE DO NOT STRIVE TO USE OUR OPINIONS ABOUT GOOD AND EVIL

Where is the good? In the will. Where is the evil? In the will. Where is neither of them? In those things which are independent of the will. Well then? Does any one among us think of these lessons out of the schools? Does any one meditate (strive) by himself to give an answer to things as in the case of questions?—Is it day?—Yes.—Is it night?—No.—Well, is the number of stars even?—I cannot say.—When money is shown (offered) to you, have you studied to make the proper answer, that money is not a good thing? Have you practised yourself in these answers, or only against sophisms? Why do you wonder then if in the cases which you have studied, in those you have improved; but in those which you have not studied, in those you remain the same? When the rhetorician knows that he has written well, that he has committed to memory what he has written, and brings an agreeable voice, why is he still anxious? Because he is not satisfied with having studied. What then does he want? To be praised by the audience? For the purpose then of being able to practise declamation he has been disciplined; but with respect to praise and blame he has not been disciplined. For when did he hear from any one what praise is, what blame is, what the nature of each is, what kind of praise should be sought, or what kind of blame should be shunned? And when did he practise this discipline which follows these words (things)? Why then do you still wonder, if in the matters which a man has learned, there he surpasses others, and in those in which he has not been disciplined, there he is the same with the many. So the lute player knows how to play, sings well, and has a fine dress, and yet he trembles when he enters on the stage; for these matters he understands, but he does not know what a crowd is, nor the shouts of a crowd, nor what ridicule is. Neither does he know what anxiety is, whether it is our work or the work of another, whether it is possible to stop it or not. For this reason if he has been praised, he leaves the theatre puffed up, but if he has been ridiculed, the swollen bladder has been punctured and subsides.

This is the case also with ourselves. What do we admire? Externals. About what things are we busy? Externals. And have we any doubt then why we fear or why we are anxious? What then happens when we think the things, which are coming on us, to be evils? It is not in our power not to be afraid, it is not in our power not to be anxious. Then we say, Lord God, how shall I not be anxious? Fool, have you not hands, did not God make them for you? Sit down now and pray that your nose may not run. Wipe yourself rather and do not blame him. Well then, has he given to you nothing in the present case? Has he not given to you endurance? Has he not given to you magnanimity? Has he not given to you manliness? When you have such hands do you still look for one who shall wipe your nose? But we neither study these things nor care for them. Give me a man who cares how he shall do anything, not for the obtaining of a thing, but who cares about his own energy. What man, when he is walking about, cares for his own energy? Who, when he is deliberating, cares about his own deliberation, and not about obtaining that about which he deliberates? And if he succeeds, he is elated and says, How well we have deliberated; did I not tell you, brother, that it is impossible, when we have thought about anything, that it should not turn out thus? But if the thing should turn out otherwise, the wretched man is humbled; he knows not even what to say about what has taken place. Who among us for the sake of this matter has consulted a seer? Who among us as to his actions has not slept in indifference? Who? Give (name) to me one that I may see the man whom I have long been looking for, who is truly noble and ingenuous, whether young or old; name him.

What then are the things which are heavy on us and disturb us? What else than opinions? What else than opinions lies heavy upon him who goes away and leaves his companions and friends and places and habits of life? Now little children, for instance, when they cry on the nurse leaving them for a short time, forget their sorrow if they receive a small cake. Do you choose then that we should compare you to little children? No, by Zeus, for I do not wish to be pacified by a small cake, but by right opinions. And what are these? Such as a man ought to study all day, and not to be affected by anything that is not his own, neither by companion nor place nor gymnasia, and not even by his own body, but to remember the law and to have it before his eyes. And what is the divine law? To keep a man's own, not to claim that which belongs to others, but to use what is given, and when it is not given, not to desire it; and when a thing is taken away, to give it up readily and immediately, and to be thankful for the time that a man has had the use of it, if you would not cry for your nurse and mamma. For what matter does it make by what thing a man is subdued, and on what he depends? In what respect are you better than he who cries for a girl, if you grieve for a little gymnasium, and little porticos, and young men, and such places of amusement? Another comes and laments that he shall no longer drink the water of Dirce. Is the Marcian water worse than that of Dirce? But I was used to the water of Dirce. And you in turn will be used to the other. Then if you become attached to this also, cry for this too, and try to make a verse like the verse of Euripides,

The hot baths of Nero and the Marcian water.

See how tragedy is made when common things happen to silly men.

When then shall I see Athens again and the Acropolis? Wretch, are you not content with what you see daily? Have you anything better or greater to see than the sun, the moon, the stars, the whole earth, the sea? But if indeed you comprehend Him who administers the whole, and carry him about in yourself, do you still desire small stones and a beautiful rock?

HOW WE MUST ADAPT PRECONCEPTIONS TO PARTICULAR CASES

What is the first business of him who philosophizes? To throw away self-conceit (Greek: *oiaesis*). For it is impossible for a man to begin to learn that which he thinks that he knows. As to things then which ought to be done and ought not to be done, and good and bad, and beautiful and ugly, all of us talking of them at random go to the philosophers; and on these matters we praise, we censure, we accuse, we blame, we judge and determine about principles honorable and dishonorable. But why do we go to the philosophers? Because we wish to learn what we do not think that we know. And what is this? Theorems. For we wish to learn what philosophers say as being something elegant and acute; and some wish to learn that they may get profit from what they learn. It is ridiculous then to think that a person wishes to learn one thing, and will learn another; or further, that a man will make proficiency in that which he does not learn. But the many are deceived by this which deceived also the rhetorician Theopompus, when he blames even Plato for wishing everything to be defined. For what does he say? Did none of us before you use the words good or just, or do we utter the sounds in an unmeaning and empty way without understanding what they severally signify? Now who tells you, Theopompus, that we had not natural notions of each of these things and preconceptions (Greek: *prolaepseis*)? But it is not possible to adapt preconceptions to their correspondent objects if we have not distinguished (analyzed) them, and inquired what object must be subjected to each preconception. You may make the same charge against physicians also. For who among us did not use the words healthy and unhealthy before Hippocrates lived, or did we utter these words as empty sounds? For we have also a certain preconception of health, but we are not able to adapt it. For this reason one says, Abstain from food; another says, Give food; another says, Bleed; and another says, Use cupping. What is the reason? is it any other than that a man cannot properly adapt the preconceptions of health to particulars?

HOW WE SHOULD STRUGGLE AGAINST APPEARANCES

Every habit and faculty is maintained and increased by the corresponding actions: the habit of walking by walking, the habit of running by running. If you would be a good reader, read; if a writer, write. But when you shall not have read for thirty days in succession, but have done something else, you will know the consequence. In the same way, if you shall have lain down ten days, get up and attempt to make a long walk, and you will see how your legs are weakened. Generally then if you would make anything a habit, do it; if you would not make it a habit, do not do it, but accustom yourself to do something else in place of it.

So it is with respect to the affections of the soul: when you have been angry, you must know that not only has this evil befallen you, but that you have also increased the habit, and in a manner thrown fuel upon fire.

In this manner certainly, as philosophers say, also diseases of the mind grow up. For when you have once desired money, if reason be applied to lead to a perception of the evil, the desire is stopped, and the ruling faculty of our mind is restored to the original authority. But if you apply no means of cure, it no longer returns to the same state, but being again excited by the corresponding appearance, it is inflamed to desire quicker than before: and when this takes place continually, it is henceforth hardened (made callous), and the disease of the mind confirms the love of money. For he who has had a fever, and has been relieved from it, is not in the same state that he was before, unless he has been completely cured. Something of the kind happens also in diseases of the soul. Certain traces and blisters are left in it, and unless a man shall completely efface them, when he is again lashed on the same places, the lash will produce not blisters (weals) but sores. If then you wish not to be of an angry temper, do not feed the habit: throw nothing on it which will increase it: at first keep quiet, and count the days on which you have not been angry. I used to be in passion every day; now every second day; then every third, then every fourth. But if you have intermitted thirty days, make a sacrifice to God. For the habit at first begins to be weakened, and then is completely destroyed. "I have not been vexed to-day, nor the day after, nor yet on any succeeding day during two or three months; but I took care when some exciting things happened." Be assured that you are in a good way.

How then shall this be done? Be willing at length to be approved by yourself, be willing to appear beautiful to God, desire to be in purity with your own pure self and with God. Then when any such appearance visits you, Plato says, Have recourse to expiations, go a suppliant to the temples of the averting deities. It is even sufficient if you resort to the society of noble and just men, and compare yourself with them, whether you find one who is living or dead.

But in the first place, be not hurried away by the rapidity of the appearance, but say, Appearances, wait for me a little; let me see who you are, and what you are about; let me put you to the test. And then do not allow the appearance to lead you on and draw lively pictures of the things which will follow; for if you do, it will carry you off wherever it pleases. But rather bring in to oppose it some other beautiful and noble appearance, and cast out this base appearance. And if you are accustomed to be exercised in this way, you will see what shoulders, what sinews, what strength you have. But now it is only trifling words, and nothing more.

This is the true athlete, the man who exercises himself against such appearances. Stay, wretch, do not be carried away. Great is the combat, divine is the work; it is for kingship, for freedom, for happiness, for freedom from perturbation. Remember God; call on him as a helper and protector, as men at sea call on the Dioscuri in a storm. For what is a greater storm than that which comes from appearances which are violent and drive away the reason? For the storm itself, what else is it but an appearance? For take away the fear of death, and suppose as many thunders and lightnings as you please, and you will know what calm and serenity there is in the ruling faculty. But if you have once been defeated and say that you will conquer hereafter, and then say the same again, be assured that you will at last be in so wretched a condition and so weak that you will not even know afterwards that you are doing wrong, but you will even begin to make apologies (defences) for your wrong-doing, and then you will confirm the saying of Hesiod to be true,

With constant ills the dilatory strives.

OF INCONSISTENCY

Some things men readily confess, and other things they do not. No one then will confess that he is a fool or without understanding; but quite the contrary you will hear all men saying, I wish that I had fortune equal to my understanding. But men readily confess that they are timid, and they say: I am rather timid, I confess; but as to other respects you will not find me to be foolish. A man will not readily confess that he is intemperate; and that he is unjust, he will not confess at all. He will by no means confess that he is envious or a busybody. Most men will confess that they are compassionate. What then is the reason?

The chief thing (the ruling thing) is inconsistency and confusion in the things which relate to good and evil. But different men have different reasons; and generally what they imagine to be base, they do not confess at all. But they suppose timidity to be a characteristic of a good disposition, and compassion also; but silliness to be the absolute characteristic of a slave. And they do not at all admit (confess) the things which are offences against society. But in the case of most errors for this reason chiefly they are induced to confess them, because they imagine that there is something involuntary in them as in timidity and compassion; and if a man confess that he is in any respect intemperate, he alleges love (or passion) as an excuse for what is involuntary. But men do not imagine injustice to be at all involuntary. There is also in jealousy, as they suppose, something involuntary; and for this reason they confess to jealousy also.

Living then among such men, who are so confused, so ignorant of what they say, and of the evils which they have or have not, and why they have them, or how they shall be relieved of them, I think it is worth the trouble for a man to watch constantly (and to ask) whether I also am one of them, what imagination I have about myself, how I conduct myself, whether I conduct myself as a prudent man, whether I conduct myself as a temperate man, whether I ever say this, that I have been taught to be prepared for everything that may happen. Have I the consciousness, which a man who knows nothing ought to have, that I know nothing? Do I go to my teacher as men go to oracles, prepared to obey? or do I like a snivelling boy go to my school to learn history and understand the books which I did not understand before, and, if it should happen so, to explain them also to others? Man, you have had a fight in the house with a poor slave, you have turned the family upside down, you have frightened the neighbors, and you come to me as if you were a wise man, and you take your seat and judge how I have explained some word, and how I have babbled whatever came into my head. You come full of envy, and humbled, because you bring nothing from home; and you sit during the discussion thinking of nothing else than how your father is disposed towards you and your brother. What are they saying about me there? now they think that I am improving, and are saying, He will return with all knowledge. I wish I could learn everything before I return; but much labor is necessary, and no one sends me anything, and the baths at Nicopolis are dirty; everything is bad at home, and bad here.

ON FRIENDSHIP

What a man applies himself to earnestly, that he naturally loves. Do men then apply themselves earnestly to the things which are bad? By no means. Well, do they apply themselves to things which in no way concern themselves? Not to these either. It remains then that they employ themselves earnestly only about things which are good; and if they are earnestly employed about things, they love such things also. Whoever then understands what is good can also know how to love; but he who cannot distinguish good from bad, and things which are neither good nor bad from both, how can he possess the power of loving? To love, then, is only in the power of the wise.

For universally, be not deceived, every animal is attached to nothing so much as to its own interests. Whatever then appears to it an impediment to this interest, whether this be a brother, or a father, or a child, or beloved, or lover, it hates, spurns, curses; for its nature is to love nothing so much as its own interests: this is father, and brother, and kinsman, and country, and God. When then the gods appear to us to be an impediment to this, we abuse them and throw down their statues and burn their temples, as Alexander ordered the temples of Aesculapius to be burned when his dear friend died.

For this reason, if a man put in the same place his interest, sanctity, goodness, and country, and parents, and friends, all these are secured: but if he puts in one place his interest, in another his friends, and his country and his kinsmen and justice itself, all these give way, being borne down by the weight of interest. For where the I and the Mine are placed, to that place of necessity the animal inclines; if in the flesh, there is the ruling power; if in the will, it is there; and if it is in externals, it is there. If then I am there where my will is, then only shall I be a friend such as I ought to be, and son, and father; for this will be my interest, to maintain the character of fidelity, of modesty, of patience, of abstinence, of active co-operation, of observing my relations (towards all). But if I put myself in one place, and honesty in another, then the doctrine of Epicurus becomes strong, which asserts either that there is no honesty or it is that which opinion holds to be honest (virtuous).

It was through this ignorance that the Athenians and the Lacedaemonians quarrelled, and the Thebans with both; and the great king quarrelled with Hellas, and the Macedonians with both: and the Romans with the Getae. And still earlier the Trojan war happened for these reasons. Alexander was the guest of Menelaus, and if any man had seen their friendly disposition, he would not have believed any one who said that they were not friends. But there was cast between them (as between dogs) a bit of meat, a handsome woman, and about her war arose. And now when you see brothers to be friends appearing to have one mind, do not conclude from this anything about their friendship, not even if they swear it and say that it is impossible for them to be separated from one another. For the ruling principle of a bad man cannot be trusted; it is insecure, has no certain rule by which it is directed, and is overpowered at different times by different appearances. But examine, not what other men examine, if they are born of the same parents and brought up together, and under the same pedagogue; but examine this only, wherein they place their interest, whether in externals or in the will. If in externals, do not name them friends, no more than name them trustworthy or constant, or brave or free; do not name them even men, if you have any judgment. For that is not a principle of human nature which makes them bite one another, and abuse one another, and occupy deserted places or public places, as if they were mountains, and in the courts of justice display the acts of robbers; nor yet that which makes them intemperate and adulterers and corrupters, nor that which makes them do whatever else men do against one another through this one opinion only, that of placing themselves and their interests in the things which are not within the power of their will. But if you hear that in truth these men think the good to be only there, where will is, and where there is a right use of appearances, no longer trouble yourself whether they are father or son, or brothers, or have associated a long time and are companions, but when you have ascertained this only, confidently declare that they are friends, as you declare that they are faithful, that they are just. For where else is friendship than where there is fidelity, and modesty, where there is a communion of honest things and of nothing else.

But you may say, Such a one treated me with regard so long; and did he not love me? How do you know, slave, if he did not regard you in the same way as he wipes his shoes with a sponge, or as he takes care of his beast? How do you know, when you have ceased to be useful as a vessel, he will not throw you away like a broken platter? But this woman is my wife, and we have lived together so long. And how long did Eriphyle live with Amphiaraus, and was the mother of children and of many? But a necklace came between them: and what is a necklace? It is the opinion about such things. That was the bestial principle, that was the thing which broke asunder the friendship between husband and wife, that which did not allow the woman to be a wife nor the mother to be a mother. And let every man among you who has seriously resolved either to be a friend himself or to have another for his friend, cut out these opinions, hate them, drive them from his soul. And thus first of all he will not reproach himself, he will not be at variance with himself, he will not change his mind, he will not torture himself. In the next place, to another also, who is like himself, he will be altogether and completely a friend. But he will bear with the man who is unlike himself, he will be kind to him, gentle, ready to pardon on account of his ignorance, on account of his being mistaken in things of the greatest importance; but he will be harsh to no man, being well convinced of Plato's doctrine that every mind is deprived of truth unwillingly. If you cannot do this, yet you can do in all other respects as friends do, drink together, and lodge together, and sail together, and you may be born of the same parents, for snakes also are: but neither will they be friends, nor you, so long as you retain these bestial and cursed opinions.

ON THE POWER OF SPEAKING

Every man will read a book with more pleasure or even with more ease, if it is written in fairer characters. Therefore every man will also listen more readily to what is spoken, if it is signified by appropriate and becoming words. We must not say then that there is no faculty of expression: for this affirmation is the characteristic of an impious and also of a timid man. Of an impious man, because he undervalues the gifts which come from God, just as if he would take away the commodity of the power of vision, or hearing, or of seeing. Has then God given you eyes to no purpose? and to no purpose has he infused into them a spirit so strong and of such skilful contrivance as to reach a long way and to fashion the forms of things which are seen? What messenger is so swift and vigilant? And to no purpose has he made the interjacent atmosphere so efficacious and elastic that the vision penetrates through the atmosphere which is in a manner moved? And to no purpose has he made light, without the presence of which there would be no use in any other thing?

Man, be neither ungrateful for these gifts nor yet forget the things which are superior to them. But indeed for the power of seeing and hearing, and indeed for life itself, and for the things which contribute to support it, for the fruits which are dry, and for wine and oil give thanks to God: but remember that he has given you something else better than all these, I mean the power of using them, proving them, and estimating the value of each. For what is that which gives information about each of these powers, what each of them is worth? Is it each faculty itself? Did you ever hear the faculty of vision saying anything about itself? or the faculty of hearing? or wheat, or barley, or a horse, or a dog? No; but they are appointed as ministers and slaves to serve the faculty which has the power of making use of the appearances of things. And if you inquire what is the value of each thing, of whom do you inquire? who answers you? How then can any other faculty be more powerful than this, which uses the rest as ministers and itself proves each and pronounces about them? for which of them knows what itself is, and what is its own value? which of them knows when it ought to employ itself and when not? what faculty is it which opens and closes the eyes, and turns them away from objects to which it ought not to apply them and does apply them to other objects? Is it the faculty of vision? No, but it is the faculty of the will. What is that faculty which closes and opens the ears? what is that by which they are curious and inquisitive, or on the contrary unmoved by what is said? is it the faculty of hearing? It is no other than the faculty of the will. Will this faculty then, seeing that it is amidst all the other faculties which are blind and dumb and unable to see anything else except the very acts for which they are appointed in order to minister to this (faculty) and serve it, but this faculty alone sees sharp and sees what is the value of each of the rest; will this faculty declare to us that anything else is the best, or that itself is? And what else does the eye do when it is opened than see? But whether we ought to look on the wife of a certain person, and in what manner, who tells us? The faculty of the will. And whether we ought to believe what is said or not to believe it, and if we do believe, whether we ought to be moved by it or not, who tells us? Is it not the faculty of the will?

But if you ask me what then is the most excellent of all things, what must I say? I cannot say the power of speaking, but the power of the will, when it is right (Greek: *orthae*). For it is this which uses the other (the power of speaking), and all the other faculties both small and great. For when this faculty of the will is set right, a man who is not good becomes good: but when it fails, a man becomes bad. It is through this that we are unfortunate, that we are fortunate, that we blame one another, are pleased with one another. In a word, it is this which if we neglect it makes unhappiness, and if we carefully look after it, makes happiness.

What then is usually done? Men generally act as a traveller would do on his way to his own country, when he enters a good inn, and being pleased with it should remain there. Man, you have forgotten your purpose: you were not travelling to this inn, but you were passing through it. But this is a pleasant inn. And how many other inns are pleasant? and how many meadows are pleasant? yet only for passing through. But your purpose is this, to return to your country, to relieve your kinsmen of anxiety, to discharge the duties of a citizen, to marry, to beget children, to fill the usual magistracies. For you are not come to select more pleasant places, but to live in these where you were born and of which you were made a citizen. Something of the kind takes place in the matter which we are considering. Since by the aid of speech and such communication as you receive here you must advance to perfection, and purge your will and correct the faculty which makes use of the appearances of things; and since it is necessary also for the teaching (delivery) of theorems to be effected by a certain mode of expression and with a certain variety and sharpness, some persons captivated by these very things abide in them, one captivated by the expression, another by syllogisms, another again by sophisms, and still another by some other inn (Greek: *paudocheiou*) of the kind; and there they stay and waste away as they were among sirens.

Man, your purpose (business) was to make yourself capable of using conformably to nature the appearances presented to you, in your desires not to be frustrated, in your aversion from things not to fall into that which you would avoid, never to have no luck (as one may say), nor ever to have bad luck, to be free, not hindered, not compelled, conforming yourself to the administration of Zeus, obeying it, well satisfied with this, blaming no one, charging no one with fault, able from your whole soul to utter these verses:

Lead me, O Zeus, and thou too Destiny

TO (OR AGAINST) A PERSON WHO WAS ONE OF THOSE WHO WERE NOT VALUED (ESTEEMED) BY HIM

A certain person said to him (Epictetus): Frequently I desired to hear you and came to you, and you never gave me any answer; and now, if it is possible, I entreat you to say something to me. Do you think, said Epictetus, that as there is an art in anything else, so there is also an art in speaking, and that he who has the art, will speak skilfully, and he who has not, will speak unskilfully?—I do think so.—He then who by speaking receives benefit himself, and is able to benefit others, will speak skilfully; but he who is rather damaged by speaking and does damage to others, will he be unskilled in this art of speaking? And you may find that some are damaged and others benefited by speaking. And are all who hear benefited by what they hear? Or will you find that among them also some are benefited and some damaged? There are both among these also, he said. In this case also then those who hear skilfully are benefited, and those who hear unskilfully are damaged? He admitted this. Is there then a skill in hearing also, as there is in speaking? It seems so. If you choose, consider the matter in this way also. The practice of music, to whom does it belong? To a musician. And the proper making of a statue, to whom do you think that it belongs? To a statuary. And the looking at a statue skilfully, does this appear to you to require the aid of no art? This also requires the aid of art. Then if speaking properly is the business of the skilful man, do you see that to hear also with benefit is the business of the skilful man? Now as to speaking and hearing perfectly, and usefully, let us for the present, if you please, say no more, for both of us are a long way from everything of the kind. But I think that every man will allow this, that he who is going to hear philosophers requires some amount of practice in hearing. Is it not so?

Why then do you say nothing to me? I can only say this to you, that he who knows not who he is, and for what purpose he exists, and what is this world, and with whom he is associated, and what things are the good and the bad, and the beautiful and the ugly, and who neither understands discourse nor demonstration, nor what is true nor what is false, and who is not able to distinguish them, will neither desire according to nature nor turn away nor move towards, nor intend (to act), nor assent, nor dissent, nor suspend his judgment: to say all in a few words, he will go about dumb and blind, thinking that he is somebody, but being nobody. Is this so now for the first time? Is it not the fact that ever since the human race existed, all errors and misfortunes have arisen through this ignorance?

This is all that I have to say to you; and I say even this not willingly. Why? Because you have not roused me. For what must I look to in order to be roused, as men who are expert in riding are roused by generous horses? Must I look to your body? You treat it disgracefully. To your dress? That is luxurious. To your behavior, to your look? That is the same as nothing. When you would listen to a philosopher, do not say to him, You tell me nothing; but only show yourself worthy of hearing or fit for hearing; and you will see how you will move the speaker.

THAT LOGIC IS NECESSARY

When one of those who were present said, Persuade me that logic is necessary, he replied, Do you wish me to prove this to you? The answer was, Yes. Then I must use a demonstrative form of speech. This was granted. How then will you know if I am cheating you by my argument? The man was silent. Do you see, said Epictetus, that you yourself are admitting that logic is necessary, if without it you cannot know so much as this, whether logic is necessary or not necessary?

OF FINERY IN DRESS

A certain young man, a rhetorician, came to see Epictetus, with his hair dressed more carefully than was usual and his attire in an ornamental style; whereupon Epictetus said, Tell me if you do not think that some dogs are beautiful and some horses, and so of all other animals. I do think so, the youth replied. Are not then some men also beautiful and others ugly? Certainly. Do we then for the same reason call each of them in the same kind beautiful, or each beautiful for something peculiar? And you will judge of this matter thus. Since we see a dog naturally formed for one thing, and a horse for another, and for another still, as an example, a nightingale, we may generally and not improperly declare each of them to be beautiful then when it is most excellent according to its nature; but since the nature of each is different, each of them seems to me to be beautiful in a different way. Is it not so? He admitted that it was. That then which makes a dog beautiful, makes a horse ugly; and that which makes a horse beautiful, makes a dog ugly, if it is true that their natures are different. It seems to be so. For I think that what makes a Pancratiast beautiful, makes a wrestler to be not good, and a runner to be most ridiculous; and he who is beautiful for the Pentathlon, is very ugly for wrestling. It is so, said he. What then makes a man beautiful? Is it that which in its kind makes both a dog and a horse beautiful? It is, he said. What then makes a dog beautiful? The possession of the excellence of a dog. And what makes a horse beautiful? The possession of the excellence of a horse. What then makes a man beautiful? Is it not the possession of the excellence of a man? And do you then, if you wish to be beautiful, young man, labor at this, the acquisition of human excellence? But what is this? Observe whom you yourself praise, when you praise many persons without partiality: do you praise the just or the unjust? The just. Whether do you praise the moderate or the immoderate? The moderate. And the temperate or the intemperate? The temperate. If then you make yourself such a person, you will know that you will make yourself beautiful; but so long as you neglect these things, you must be ugly (Greek: *aischron*), even though you contrive all you can to appear beautiful.

IN WHAT A MAN OUGHT TO BE EXERCISED WHO HAS MADE PROFICIENCY; AND THAT WE NEGLECT THE CHIEF THINGS

There are three things (topics, Greek: *topoi*) in which a man ought to exercise himself who would be wise and good. The first concerns the desires and the aversions, that a man may not fail to get what he desires, and that he may not fall into that which he does not desire. The second concerns the movements towards an object and the movements from an object, and generally in doing what a man ought to do, that he may act according to order, to reason, and not carelessly. The third thing concerns freedom from deception and rashness in judgment, and generally it concerns the assents (Greek: *sugchatatheseis*). Of these topics the chief and the most urgent is that which relates to the affects (Greek: *ta pathae*; perturbations); for an affect is produced in no other way than by a failing to obtain that which a man desires or falling into that which a man would wish to avoid. This is that which brings in perturbations, disorders, bad fortune, misfortunes, sorrows, lamentations, and envy; that which makes men envious and jealous; and by these causes we are unable even to listen to the precepts of reason. The second topic concerns the duties of a man; for I ought not to be free from affects (Greek: *apathae*) like a statue, but I ought to maintain the relations (Greek: *scheseis*) natural and acquired, as a pious man, as a son, as a father, as a citizen.

The third topic is that which immediately concerns those who are making proficiency, that which concerns the security of the other two, so that not even in sleep any appearance unexamined may surprise us, nor in intoxication, nor in melancholy. This, it may be said, is above our power. But the present philosophers neglecting the first topic and the second (the affects and duties), employ themselves on the third, using sophistical arguments (Greek: *metapiptontas*), making conclusions from questioning, employing hypotheses, lying. For a man must, it is said, when employed on these matters, take care that he is not deceived. Who must? The wise and good man. This then is all that is wanting to you. Have you successfully worked out the rest? Are you free from deception in the matter of money? If you see a beautiful girl do you resist the appearance? If your neighbor obtains an estate by will, are you not vexed? Now is there nothing else wanting to you except unchangeable firmness of mind (Greek: *ametaptosia*)? Wretch, you hear these very things with fear and anxiety that some person may despise you, and with inquiries about what any person may say about you. And if a man come and tell you that in a certain conversation in which the question was, Who is the best philosopher, a man who was present said that a certain person was the chief philosopher, your little soul which was only a finger's length stretches out to two cubits. But if another who is present says, You are mistaken; it is not worth while to listen to a certain person, for what does he know? he has only the first principles, and no more? then you are confounded, you grow pale, you cry out immediately, I will show him who I am, that I am a great philosopher. It is seen by these very things: why do you wish to show it by others? Do you not know that Diogenes pointed out one of the sophists in this way by stretching out his middle finger? And then when the man was wild with rage, This, he said, is the certain person:

I have pointed him out to you. For a man is not shown by the finger, as a stone or a piece of wood; but when any person shows the man's principles, then he shows him as a man.

Let us look at your principles also. For is it not plain that you value not at all your own will (Greek: *proairesis*), but you look externally to things which are independent of your will? For instance, what will a certain person say? and what will people think of you? Will you be considered a man of learning; have you read Chrysippus or Antipater? for if you have read Archedamus also, you have every thing (that you can desire). Why you are still uneasy lest you should not show us who you are? Would you let me tell you what manner of man you have shown us that you are? You have exhibited yourself to us as a mean fellow, querulous, passionate, cowardly, finding fault with everything, blaming everybody, never quiet, vain: this is what you have exhibited to us. Go away now and read Archedamus; then if a mouse should leap down and make a noise, you are a dead man. For such a death awaits you as it did—what was the man's name—Crinis; and he too was proud, because he understood Archedamus. Wretch, will you not dismiss these things that do not concern you at all? These things are suitable to those who are able to learn them without perturbation, to those who can say: "I am not subject to anger, to grief, to envy: I am not hindered, I am not restrained. What remains for me? I have leisure, I am tranquil: let us see how we must deal with sophistical arguments; let us see how when a man has accepted an hypothesis he shall not be led away to anything absurd." To them such things belong. To those who are happy it is appropriate to light a fire, to dine; if they choose, both to sing and to dance. But when the vessel is sinking, you come to me and hoist the sails.

WHAT IS THE MATTER ON WHICH A GOOD MAN SHOULD BE EMPLOYED, AND IN WHAT WE OUGHT CHIEFLY TO PRACTISE OURSELVES

The material for the wise and good man is his own ruling faculty: and the body is the material for the physician and the aliptes (the man who oils persons); the land is the matter for the husbandman. The business of the wise and good man is to use appearances conformably to nature: and as it is the nature of every soul to assent to the truth, to dissent from the false, and to remain in suspense as to that which is uncertain; so it is its nature to be moved towards the desire for the good, and to aversion from the evil; and with respect to that which is neither good nor bad it feels indifferent. For as the money-changer (banker) is not allowed to reject Caesar's coin, nor the seller of herbs, but if you show the coin, whether he chooses or not, he must give up what is sold for the coin; so it is also in the matter of the soul. When the good appears, it immediately attracts to itself; the evil repels from itself. But the soul will never reject the manifest appearance of the good, any more than persons will reject Caesar's coin. On this principle depends every movement both of man and God.

Against (or with respect to) this kind of thing chiefly a man should exercise himself. As soon as you go out in the morning, examine every man whom you see, every man whom you hear; answer as to a question, What have you seen? A handsome man or woman? Apply the rule. Is this independent of the will, or dependent? Independent. Take it away. What have you seen? A man lamenting over the death of a child. Apply the rule. Death is a thing independent of the will. Take it away. Has the proconsul met you? Apply the rule. What kind of a thing is a proconsul's office? Independent of the will or dependent on it? Independent. Take this away also; it does not stand examination; cast it away; it is nothing to you.

If we practised this and exercised ourselves in it daily from morning to night, something indeed would be done. But now we are forthwith caught half asleep by every appearance, and it is only, if ever, that in the school we are roused a little. Then when we go out, if we see a man lamenting, we say, He is undone. If we see a consul, we say, He is happy. If we see an exiled man, we say, He is miserable. If we see a poor man, we say, He is wretched; he has nothing to eat.

We ought then to eradicate these bad opinions, and to this end we should direct all our efforts. For what is weeping and lamenting? Opinion. What is bad fortune? Opinion. What is civil sedition, what is divided opinion, what is blame, what is accusation, what is impiety, what is trifling? All these things are opinions, and nothing more, and opinions about things independent of the will, as if they were good and bad. Let a man transfer these opinions to things dependent on the will, and I engage for him that he will be firm and constant, whatever may be the state of things around him. Such as is a dish of water, such is the soul. Such as is the ray of light which falls on the water, such are the appearances. When the water is moved, the ray also seems to be moved, yet it is not moved. And when then a man is seized with giddiness, it is not the arts and the virtues which are confounded, but the spirit (the nervous power) on which they are impressed; but if the spirit be restored to its settled state, those things also are restored.

MISCELLANEOUS

When some person asked him how it happened that since reason has been more cultivated by the men of the present age, the progress made in former times was greater. In what respect, he answered, has it been more cultivated now, and in what respect was the progress greater then? For in that in which it has now been more cultivated, in that also the progress will now be found. At present it has been cultivated for the purpose of resolving syllogisms, and progress is made. But in former times it was cultivated for the purpose of maintaining the governing faculty in a condition conformable to nature, and progress was made. Do not then mix things which are different, and do not expect, when you are laboring at one thing to make progress in another. But see if any man among us when he is intent upon this, the keeping himself in a state conformable to nature and living so always, does not make progress. For you will not find such a man.

It is not easy to exhort weak young men; for neither is it easy to hold (soft) cheese with a hook. But those who have a good natural disposition, even if you try to turn them aside, cling still more to reason.

TO THE ADMINISTRATOR OF THE FREE CITIES WHO WAS AN EPICUREAN

When the administrator came to visit him, and the man was an Epicurean, Epictetus said, It is proper for us who are not philosophers to inquire of you who are philosophers, as those who come to a strange city inquire of the citizens and those who are acquainted with it, what is the best thing in the world, in order that we also after inquiry may go in quest of that which is best and look at it, as strangers do with the things in cities. For that there are three things which relate to man—soul, body, and things external, scarcely any man denies. It remains for you philosophers to answer what is the best. What shall we say to men? Is the flesh the best? and was it for this that Maximus sailed as far as Cassiope in winter (or bad weather) with his son, and accompanied him that he might be gratified in the flesh? When the man said that it was not, and added, Far be that from him. Is it not fit then, Epictetus said, to be actively employed about the best? It is certainly of all things the most fit. What then do we possess which is better than the flesh? The soul, he replied. And the good things of the best, are they better, or the good things of the worse? The good things of the best. And are the good things of the best within the power of the will or not within the power of the will? They are within the power of the will. Is then the pleasure of the soul a thing within the power of the will? It is, he replied. And on what shall this pleasure depend? On itself? But that cannot be conceived; for there must first exist a certain substance or nature (Greek: *ousia*) of good, by obtaining which we shall have pleasure in the soul. He assented to this also. On what then shall we depend for this pleasure of the soul? for if it shall depend on things of the soul, the substance (nature) of the good is discovered; for good cannot be one thing, and that at which we are rationally delighted another thing; nor if that which precedes is not good, can that which comes after be good, for in order that the thing which comes after may be good, that which precedes must be good. But you would not affirm this, if you are in your right mind, for you would then say what is inconsistent both with Epicurus and the rest of your doctrines. It remains then that the pleasure of the soul is in the pleasure from things of the body; and again that those bodily things must be the things which precede and the substance (nature) of the good.

Seek for doctrines which are consistent with what I say, and by making them your guide you will with pleasure abstain from things which have such persuasive power to lead us and overpower us. But if to the persuasive power of these things, we also devise such a philosophy as this which helps to push us on towards them and strengthens us to this end, what will be the consequence? In a piece of toreutic art which is the best part? the silver or the workmanship? The substance of the hand is the flesh; but the work of the hand is the principal part (that which precedes and leads the rest). The duties then are also three: those which are directed towards the existence of a thing; those which are directed towards its existence in a particular kind; and third, the chief or leading things themselves. So also in man we ought not to value the material, the poor flesh, but the principal (leading things, Greek: *ta proaegoumena*). What are these? Engaging in public business, marrying, begetting children, venerating God, taking care of parents, and generally, having desires, aversions (Greek: *echchlinein*), pursuits of things and avoidances, in the way in which we ought to do these things, and according to our nature. And how are we constituted by nature? Free, noble, modest; for what other animal blushes? what other is capable of receiving the appearance (the impression) of shame? and we are so constituted by nature as to subject pleasure to these things, as a minister, a servant, in order that it may call forth our activity, in order that it may keep us constant in acts which are conformable to nature.

HOW WE MUST EXERCISE OURSELVES AGAINST APPEARANCES (GREEK: *PHANTASIAS*)

As we exercise ourselves against sophistical questions, so we ought to exercise ourselves daily against appearances; for these appearances also propose questions to us. A certain person's son is dead. Answer; the thing is not within the power of the will: it is not an evil. A father has disinherited a certain son. What do you think of it? It is a thing beyond the power of the will, not an evil. Caesar has condemned a person. It is a thing beyond the power of the will, not an evil. The man is afflicted at this. Affliction is a thing which depends on the will: it is an evil. He has borne the condemnation bravely. That is a thing within the power of the will: it is a good. If we train ourselves in this manner, we shall make progress; for we shall never assent to anything of which there is not an appearance capable of being comprehended. Your son is dead. What has happened? Your son is dead. Nothing more? Nothing. Your ship is lost. What has happened? Your ship is lost. A man has been led to prison. What has happened? He has been led to prison. But that herein he has fared badly, every man adds from his own opinion. But Zeus, you say, does not do right in these matters. Why? because he has made you capable of endurance? because he has made you magnanimous? because he has taken from that which befalls you the power of being evils? because it is in your power to be happy while you are suffering what you suffer? because he has opened the door to you, when things do not please you? Man, go out and do not complain!

Hear how the Romans feel towards philosophers, if you would like to know. Italicus, who was the most in repute of the philosophers, once when I was present, being vexed with his own friends and as if he was suffering something intolerable, said: "I cannot bear it, you are killing me; you will make me such as that man is," pointing to me.

TO A CERTAIN RHETORICIAN WHO WAS GOING UP TO ROME ON A SUIT

When a certain person came to him, who was going up to Rome on account of a suit which had regard to his rank, Epictetus inquired the reason of his going to Rome, and the man then asked what he thought about the matter. Epictetus replied: If you ask me what you will do in Rome, whether you will succeed or fail, I have no rule (Greek: *theoraema*) about this. But if you ask me how you will fare, I can tell you: if you have right opinions (Greek: *dogmata*), you will fare well; if they are false, you will fare ill. For to every man the cause of his acting is opinion. For what is the reason why you desired to be elected governor of the Cnossians? Your opinion. What is the reason that you are now going up to Rome? Your opinion. And going in winter, and with danger and expense? I must go. What tells you this? Your opinion. Then if opinions are the causes of all actions, and a man has bad opinions, such as the cause may be, such also is the effect! Have we then all sound opinions, both you and your adversary? And how do you differ? But have you sounder opinions than your adversary? Why? You think so. And so does he think that his opinions are better; and so do madmen. This is a bad criterion. But show to me that you have made some inquiry into your opinions and have taken some pains about them. And as now you are sailing to Rome in order to become governor of the Cnossians, and you are not content to stay at home with the honors which you had, but you desire something greater and more conspicuous, so when did you ever make a voyage for the purpose of examining your own opinions, and casting them out, if you have any that are bad? Whom have you approached for this purpose? What time have you fixed for it? What age? Go over the times of your life by yourself, if you are ashamed of me (knowing the fact) when you were a boy, did you examine your own opinions? and did you not then, as you do all things now, do as you did do? and when you were become a youth and attended the rhetoricians, and yourself practised rhetoric, what did you imagine that you were deficient in? And when you were a young man and engaged in public matters, and pleaded causes yourself, and were gaining reputation, who then seemed your equal? And when would you have submitted to any man examining and showing that your opinions are bad? What then do you wish me to say to you? Help me in this matter. I have no theorem (rule) for this. Nor have you, if you came to me for this purpose, come to me as a philosopher, but as to a seller of vegetables or a shoemaker. For what purpose then have philosophers theorems? For this purpose, that whatever may happen, our ruling faculty may be and continue to be conformable to nature. Does this seem to you a small thing? No; but the greatest. What then? does it need only a short time? and is it possible to seize it as you pass by? If you can, seize it.

Then you will say, I met with Epictetus as I should meet with a stone or a statue: for you saw me and nothing more. But he meets with a man as a man, who learns his opinions, and in his turn shows his own. Learn my opinions: show me yours; and then say that you have visited me. Let us examine one another: if I have any bad opinion, take it away; if you have any, show it. This is the meaning of meeting with a philosopher. Not so (you say): but this is only a passing visit, and while we are hiring the vessel, we can also see Epictetus. Let us see what he says. Then you go away and say: Epictetus was nothing; he used solecisms and spoke in a barbarous way. For of what else do you come as judges? Well, but a man may say to me, if I attend to such matters (as you do), I shall have no land as you have none; I shall have no silver cups as you have none, nor fine beasts as you have none. In answer to tins it is perhaps sufficient to say: I have no need of such things; but if you possess many things you have need of others: whether you choose or not, you are poorer than I am. What then have I need of? Of that which you have not? of firmness, of a mind which is conformable to nature, of being free from perturbation.

IN WHAT MANNER WE OUGHT TO BEAR SICKNESS

When the need of each opinion comes, we ought to have it in readiness: on the occasion of breakfast, such opinions as relate to breakfast; in the bath, those that concern the bath; in bed, those that concern bed.

> Let sleep not come upon thy languid eyes Before each daily action thou hast scann'd; What's done amiss, what done, what left undone; From first to last examine all, and then Blame what is wrong, in what is right rejoice.

And we ought to retain these verses in such way that we may use them, not that we may utter them aloud, as when we exclaim, "Paean Apollo." Again in fever we should have ready such opinions as concern a fever; and we ought not, as soon as the fever begins, to lose and forget all. A man who has a fever may say: If I philosophize any longer, may I be hanged: wherever I go, I must take care of the poor body, that a fever may not come. But what is philosophizing? Is it not a preparation against events which may happen? Do you not understand that you are saying something of this kind? "If I shall still prepare myself to bear with patience what happens, may I be hanged." But this is just as if a man after receiving blows should give up the Pancratium. In the Pancratium it is in our power to desist and not to receive blows.

But in the other matter if we give up philosophy, what shall we gain? What then should a man say on the occasion of each painful thing? It was for this that I exercised myself, for this I disciplined myself. God says to you: Give me a proof that you have duly practised athletics, that you have eaten what you ought, that you have been exercised, that you have obeyed the aliptes (the oiler and rubber). Then do you show yourself weak when the time for action comes? Now is the time for the fever. Let it be borne well. Now is the time for thirst, bear it well. Now is the time for hunger, bear it well. Is it not in your power? Who shall hinder you? The physician will hinder you from drinking; but he cannot prevent you from bearing thirst well: and he will hinder you from eating; but he cannot prevent you from bearing hunger well.

But I cannot attend to my philosophical studies. And for what purpose do you follow them? Slave, is it not that you may be happy, that you may be constant, is it not that you may be in a state conformable to nature and live so? What hinders you when you have a fever from having your ruling faculty conformable to nature? Here is the proof of the thing, here is the test of the philosopher. For this also is a part of life, like walking, like sailing, like journeying by land, so also is fever. Do you read when you are walking? No. Nor do you when you have a fever. But if you walk about well, you have all that belongs to a man who walks. If you bear a fever well, you have all that belongs to a man in a fever. What is it to bear a fever well? Not to blame God or man; not to be afflicted at that which happens, to expect death well and nobly, to do what must be done: when the physician comes in, not to be frightened at what he says; nor if he says you are doing well, to be overjoyed. For what good has he told you? and when you were in health, what good was that to you? And even if he says you are in a bad way, do not despond. For what is it to be ill? is it that you are near the severance of the soul and the body? what harm is there in this? If you are not near now, will you not afterwards be near? Is the world going to be turned upside down when you are dead? Why then do you flatter the physician? Why do you say if you please, master, I shall be well? Why do you give him an opportunity of raising his eyebrows (being proud; or showing his importance)? Do you not value a physician, as you do a shoemaker when he is measuring your foot, or a carpenter when he is building your house, and so treat the physician as to the body which is not yours, but by nature dead? He who has a fever has an opportunity of doing this: if he does these things, he has what belongs to him. For it is not the business of a philosopher to look after these externals, neither his wine nor his oil nor his poor body, but his own ruling power. But as to externals how must he act? so far as not to be careless about them. Where then is there reason for fear? where is there then still reason for anger, and of fear about what belongs to others, about things which are of no value? For we ought to have these two principles in readiness, that except the will nothing is good nor bad; and that we ought not to lead events, but to follow them. My brother ought not to have behaved thus to me. No, but he will see to that; and, however he may behave, I will conduct myself towards him as I ought. For this is my own business; that belongs to another: no man can prevent this, the other thing can be hindered.

ABOUT EXERCISE

We ought not to make our exercises consist in means contrary to nature and adapted to cause admiration, for if we do so, we who call ourselves philosophers, shall not differ at all from jugglers. For it is difficult even to walk on a rope; and not only difficult, but it is also dangerous. Ought we for this reason to practice walking on a rope, or setting up a palm-tree, or embracing statues? By no means. Every thing which is difficult and dangerous is not suitable for practice; but that is suitable which conduces to the working out of that which is proposed to us. And what is that which is proposed to us as a thing to be worked out? To live with desire and aversion (avoidance of certain things) free from restraint. And what is this? Neither to be disappointed in that which you desire, nor to fall into anything which you would avoid. Towards this object then exercise (practice) ought to tend. For since it is not possible to have your desire not disappointed and your aversion free from falling into that which you would avoid, without great and constant practice, you must know that if you allow your desire and aversion to turn to things which are not within the power of the will, you will neither have your desire capable of attaining your object, nor your aversion free from the power of avoiding that which you would avoid. And since strong habit leads (prevails), and we are accustomed to employ desire and aversion only to things which are not within the power of our will, we ought to oppose to this habit a contrary habit, and where there is great slipperiness in the appearances, there to oppose the habit of exercise. Then at last, if occasion presents itself, for the purpose of trying yourself at a proper time you will descend into the arena to know if appearances overpower you as they did formerly. But at first fly far from that which is stronger than yourself; the contest is unequal between a charming young girl and a beginner in philosophy. The earthen pitcher, as the saying is, and the rock do not agree.

WHAT SOLITUDE IS, AND WHAT KIND OF PERSON A SOLITARY MAN IS

Solitude is a certain condition of a helpless man. For because a man is alone, he is not for that reason also solitary; just as though a man is among numbers, he is not therefore not solitary. When then we have lost either a brother, or a son, or a friend on whom we were accustomed to repose, we say that we are left solitary, though we are often in Rome, though such a crowd meet us, though so many live in the same place, and sometimes we have a great number of slaves. For the man who is solitary, as it is conceived, is considered to be a helpless person and exposed to those who wish to harm him. For this reason when we travel, then especially do we say that we are lonely when we fall among robbers, for it is not the sight of a human creature which removes us from solitude, but the sight of one who is faithful and modest and helpful to us. For if being alone is enough to make solitude, you may say that even Zeus is solitary in the conflagration and bewails himself saying, Unhappy that I am who have neither Hera, nor Athena, nor Apollo, nor brother, nor son, nor descendant, nor kinsman. This is what some say that he does when he is alone at the conflagration. For they do not understand how a man passes his life when he is alone, because they set out from a certain natural principle, from the natural desire of community and mutual love and from the pleasure of conversation among men. But none the less a man ought to be prepared in a manner for this also (being alone), to be able to be sufficient for himself and to be his own companion. For as Zeus dwells with himself, and is tranquil by himself, and thinks of his own administration and of its nature, and is employed in thoughts suitable to himself; so ought we also to be able to talk with ourselves, not to feel the want of others also, not to be unprovided with the means of passing our time; to observe the divine administration, and the relation of ourselves to everything else; to consider how we formerly were affected towards things that happened and how at present; what are still the things which give us pain; how these also can be cured and how removed; if any things require improvement, to improve them according to reason.

Well then, if some man should come upon me when I am alone and murder me? Fool, not murder You, but your poor body.

What kind of solitude then remains? what want? why do we make ourselves worse than children; and what do children do when they are left alone? They take up shells and ashes, and they build something, then pull it down, and build something else, and so they never want the means of passing the time. Shall I then, if you sail away, sit down and weep, because I have been left alone and solitary? Shall I then have no shells, no ashes? But children do what they do through want of thought (or deficiency in knowledge), and we through knowledge are unhappy.

Every great power (faculty) is dangerous to beginners. You must then bear such things as you are able, but conformably to nature: but not ... Practise sometimes a way of living like a person out of health that you may at some time live like a man in health.

CERTAIN MISCELLANEOUS MATTERS

As bad tragic actors cannot sing alone, but in company with many, so some persons cannot walk about alone. Man, if you are anything, both walk alone and talk to yourself, and do not hide yourself in the chorus. Examine a little at last, look around, stir yourself up, that you may know who you are.

You must root out of men these two things, arrogance (pride) and distrust. Arrogance then is the opinion that you want nothing (are deficient in nothing); but distrust is the opinion that you cannot be happy when so many circumstances surround you. Arrogance is removed by confutation; and Socrates was the first who practised this. And (to know) that the thing is not impossible inquire and seek. This search will do you no harm; and in a manner this is philosophizing, to seek how it is possible to employ desire and aversion (Greek: *echchlisis*) without impediment.

I am superior to you, for my father is a man of consular rank. Another says, I have been a tribune, but you have not. If we were horses, would you say, My father was swifter? I have much barley and fodder, or elegant neck ornaments. If then you were saying this, I said, Be it so: let us run then. Well, is there nothing in a man such as running in a horse, by which it will be known which is superior and inferior? Is there not modesty (Greek: *aidos*), fidelity, justice? Show yourself superior in these, that you may be superior as a man. If you tell me that you can kick violently, I also will say to you, that you are proud of that which is the act of an ass.

THAT WE OUGHT TO PROCEED WITH CIRCUMSPECTION TO EVERYTHING

In every act consider what precedes and what follows, and then proceed to the act. If you do not consider, you will at first begin with spirit, since you have not thought at all of the things which follow; but afterwards when some consequences have shown themselves, you will basely desist (from that which you have begun).—I wish to conquer at the Olympic games.—(And I too, by the gods; for it is a fine thing.) But consider here what precedes and what follows; and then, if it is for your good, undertake the thing. You must act according to rules, follow strict diet, abstain from delicacies, exercise yourself by compulsion at fixed times, in heat, in cold; drink no cold water, nor wine, when there is opportunity of drinking it. In a word, you must surrender yourself to the trainer, as you do to a physician. Next in the contest, you must be covered with sand, sometimes dislocate a hand, sprain an ankle, swallow a quantity of dust, be scourged with the whip; and after undergoing all this, you must sometimes be conquered. After reckoning all these things, if you have still an inclination, go to the athletic practice. If you do not reckon them, observe you will behave like children who at one time play as wrestlers, then as gladiators, then blow a trumpet, then act a tragedy, when they have seen and admired such things. So you also do: you are at one time a wrestler (athlete), then a gladiator, then a philosopher, then a rhetorician; but with your whole soul you are nothing: like the ape you imitate all that you see; and always one thing after another pleases you, but that which becomes familiar displeases you. For you have never undertaken anything after consideration, nor after having explored the whole matter and put it to a strict examination; but you have undertaken it at hazard and with a cold desire. Thus some persons having seen a philosopher and having heard one speak like Euphrates—and yet who can speak like him?—wish to be philosophers themselves.

Man, consider first what the matter is (which you propose to do), then your own nature also, what it is able to bear. If you are a wrestler, look at your shoulders, your thighs, your loins: for different men are naturally formed for different things. Do you think that, if you do (what you are doing daily), you can be a philosopher? Do you think that you can eat as you do now, drink as you do now, and in the same way be angry and out of humor? You must watch, labor, conquer certain desires, you must depart from your kinsmen, be despised by your slaves, laughed at by those who meet you, in everything you must be in an inferior condition, as to magisterial office, in honors, in courts of justice. When you have considered all these things completely, then, if you think proper, approach to philosophy, if you would gain in exchange for these things freedom from perturbations, liberty, tranquillity. If you have not considered these things, do not approach philosophy: do not act like children, at one time a philosopher, then a tax collector, then a rhetorician, then a procurator (officer) of Caesar. These things are not consistent. You must be one man either good or bad; you must either labor at your own ruling faculty or at external things; you must either labor at things within or at external things; that is, you must either occupy the place of a philosopher or that of one of the vulgar.

A person said to Rufus when Galba was murdered: Is the world now governed by Providence? But Rufus replied: Did I ever incidentally form an argument from Galba that the world is governed by Providence?

THAT WE OUGHT WITH CAUTION TO ENTER INTO FAMILIAR INTERCOURSE WITH MEN

If a man has frequent intercourse with others either for talk, or drinking together, or generally for social purposes, he must either become like them, or change them to his own fashion. For if a man places a piece of quenched charcoal close to a piece that is burning, either the quenched charcoal will quench the other, or the burning charcoal will light that which is quenched. Since then the danger is so great, we must cautiously enter into such intimacies with those of the common sort, and remember that it is impossible that a man can keep company with one who is covered with soot without being partaker of the soot himself. For what will you do if a man speaks about gladiators, about horses, about athletes, or what is worse about men? Such a person is bad, such a person is good; this was well done, this was done badly. Further, if he scoff, or ridicule, or show an ill-natured disposition? Is any man among us prepared like a lute-player when he takes a lute, so that as soon as he has touched the strings, he discovers which are discordant, and tunes the instrument? Such a power as Socrates had who in all his social intercourse could lead his companions to his own purpose? How should you have this power? It is therefore a necessary consequence that you are carried about by the common kind of people.

Why then are they more powerful than you? Because they utter these useless words from their real opinions; but you utter your elegant words only from your lips; for this reason they are without strength and dead, and it is nauseous to listen to your exhortations and your miserable virtue, which is talked of everywhere (up and down). In this way the vulgar have the advantage over you; for every opinion (Greek: *dogma*) is strong and invincible. Until then the good (Greek: *chompsai*) sentiments (Greek: *hupolaepseis*) are fixed in you, and you shall have acquired a certain power for your security, I advise you to be careful in your association with common persons; if you are not, every day like wax in the sun there will be melted away whatever you inscribe on your minds in the school. Withdraw then yourselves far from the sun so long as you have these waxen sentiments. For this reason also philosophers advise men to leave their native country, because ancient habits distract them and do not allow a beginning to be made of a different habit; nor can we tolerate those who meet us and say: See such a one is now a philosopher, who was once so and so. Thus also physicians send those who have lingering diseases to a different country and a different air; and they do right. Do you also introduce other habits than those which you have; fix you opinions and exercise yourselves in them. But you do not so; you go hence to a spectacle, to a show of gladiators, to a place of exercise (Greek: *chuston*), to a circus; then you come back hither, and again from this place you go to those places, and still the same persons. And there is no pleasing (good) habit, nor attention, nor care about self and observation of this kind. How shall I use the appearances presented to me? according to nature, or contrary to nature? how do I answer to them? as I ought, or as I ought not? Do I say to those things which are independent of the will, that they do not concern me? For if you are not yet in this state, fly from your former habits, fly from the common sort, if you intend ever to begin to be something.

ON PROVIDENCE

When you make any charge against Providence, consider, and you will learn that the thing has happened according to reason. Yes, but the unjust man has the advantage. In what? In money. Yes, for he is superior to you in this, that he flatters, is free from shame, and is watchful. What is the wonder? But see if he has the advantage over you in being faithful, in being modest; for you will not find it to be so; but wherein you are superior, there you will find that you have the advantage. And I once said to a man who was vexed because Philostorgus was fortunate: Would you choose to lie with Sura? May it never happen, he replied, that this day should come? Why then are you vexed, if he receives something in return for that which he sells; or how can you consider him happy who acquires those things by such means as you abominate; or what wrong does Providence, if he gives the better things to the better men? Is it not better to be modest than to be rich? He admitted this. Why are you vexed then, man, when you possess the better thing? Remember then always and have in readiness the truth, that this is a law of nature, that the superior has an advantage over the inferior in that in which he is superior; and you will never be vexed.

But my wife treats me badly. Well, if any man asks you what this is, say, my wife treats me badly. Is there then nothing more? Nothing. My father gives me nothing. (What is this? my father gives me nothing. Is there nothing else then? Nothing); but to say that this is an evil is something which must be added to it externally, and falsely added. For this reason we must not get rid of poverty, but of the opinion about poverty, and then we shall be happy.

ABOUT CYNICISM

When one of his pupils inquired of Epictetus, and he was a person who appeared to be inclined to Cynicism, what kind of person a Cynic ought to be, and what was the notion (Greek: *prolaepsis*) of the thing, we will inquire, said Epictetus, at leisure; but I have so much to say to you that he who without God attempts so great a matter, is hateful to God, and has no other purpose than to act indecently in public.

In the first place, in the things which relate to yourself, you must not be in any respect like what you do now; you must not blame God or man; you must take away desire altogether, you must transfer avoidance (Greek: *echchlisis*) only to the things which are within the power of the will; you must not feel anger nor resentment or envy nor pity; a girl must not appear handsome to you, nor must you love a little reputation, nor be pleased with a boy or a cake. For you ought to know that the rest of men throw walls around them and houses and darkness when they do any such things, and they have many means of concealment. A man shuts the door, he sets somebody before the chamber; if a person comes, say that he is out, he is not at leisure. But the Cynic instead of all these things must use modesty as his protection; if he does not, he will be indecent in his nakedness and under the open sky. This is his house, his door; this is the slave before his bedchamber; this is his darkness. For he ought not to wish to hide anything that he does; and if he does, he is gone, he has lost the character of a Cynic, of a man who lives under the open sky, of a free man; he has begun to fear some external thing, he has begun to have need of concealment, nor can he get concealment when he chooses. For where shall he hide himself and how? And if by chance this public instructor shall be detected, this paedagogue, what kind of things will he be compelled to suffer? when then a man fears these things, is it possible for him to be bold with his whole soul to superintend men? It cannot be: it is impossible.

In the first place then you must make your ruling faculty pure, and this mode of life also. Now (you should say), to me the matter to work on is my understanding, as wood is to the carpenter, as hides to the shoemaker; and my business is the right use of appearances. But the body is nothing to me: the parts of it are nothing to me. Death? Let it come when it chooses, either death of the whole or of a part. Fly, you say. And whither; can any man eject me out of the world? He cannot. But wherever I go, there is the sun, there is the moon, there are the stars, dreams, omens, and the conversation (Greek: *omilia*) with gods.

Then, if he is thus prepared, the true Cynic cannot be satisfied with this; but he must know that he is sent a messenger from Zeus to men about good and bad things, to show them that they have wandered and are seeking the substance of good and evil where it is not, but where it is, they never think; and that he is a spy, as Diogenes was carried off to Philip after the battle of Chaeroneia as a spy. For in fact a Cynic is a spy of the things which are good for men and which are evil, and it is his duty to examine carefully and to come and report truly, and not to be struck with terror so as to point out as enemies those who are not enemies, nor in any other way to be perturbed by appearances nor confounded.

It is his duty then to be able with a loud voice, if the occasion should arise, and appearing on the tragic stage to say like Socrates: Men, whither are you hurrying, what are you doing, wretches? like blind people you are wandering up and down; you are going by another road, and have left the true road; you seek for prosperity and happiness where they are not, and if another shows you where they are, you do not believe him. Why do you seek it without? In the body? It is not there. If you doubt, look at Myro, look at Ophellius. In possessions? It is not there. But if you do not believe me, look at Croesus: look at those who are now rich, with what lamentations their life is filled. In power? It is not there. If it is, those must be happy who have been twice and thrice consuls; but they are not. Whom shall we believe in these matters? You who from without see their affairs and are dazzled by an appearance, or the men themselves? What do they say? Hear them when they groan, when they grieve, when on account of these very consulships and glory and splendor they think that they are more wretched and in greater danger. Is it in royal power? It is not: if it were, Nero would have been happy, and Sardanapalus. But neither was Agamemnon happy, though he was a better man than Sardanapalus and Nero; but while others are snoring, what is he doing?

Much from his head he tore his rooted hair:
Iliad, x., 15.

and what does he say himself?

"I am perplexed," he says, "and
Disturb'd I am," and "my heart out of my bosom
Is leaping."
Iliad, x., 91.

Wretch, which of your affairs goes badly? Your possessions? No. Your body? No. But you are rich in gold and copper. What then is the matter with you? That part of you, whatever it is, has been neglected by you and is corrupted, the part with which we desire, with which we avoid, with which we move towards and move from things. How neglected? He knows not the nature of good for which he is made by nature and the nature of evil; and what is his own, and what belongs to another; and when anything that belongs to others goes badly, he says, Woe to me, for the Hellenes are in danger. Wretched is his ruling faculty, and alone neglected and uncared for. The Hellenes are going to die destroyed by the Trojans. And if the Trojans do not kill them, will they not die? Yes; but not all at once. What difference then does it make? For if death is an evil, whether men die altogether, or if they die singly, it is equally an evil. Is anything else then going to happen than the separation of the soul and the body? Nothing. And if the Hellenes perish, is the door closed, and is it not in your power to die? It is. Why then do you lament (and say), Oh, you are a king and have the sceptre of Zeus? An unhappy king does not exist more than an unhappy god. What then art thou? In truth a shepherd: for you weep as shepherds do, when a wolf has carried off one of their sheep: and these who are governed by you are sheep. And why did you come hither? Was your desire in any danger? was your aversion (Greek: *echchlisis*)? was your movement (pursuits)? was your avoidance of things? He replies, No; but the wife of my brother was carried off. Was it not then a great gain to be deprived of an adulterous wife? Shall we be despised then by the Trojans? What kind of people are the Trojans, wise or foolish? If they are wise, why do you fight with them? If they are fools, why do you care about them?

Do you possess the body then free or is it in servile condition? We do not know. Do you not know that it is the slave of fever, of gout, ophthalmia, dysentery, of a tyrant, of fire, of iron, of everything which is stronger? Yes, it is a slave. How then is it possible that anything which belongs to the body can be free from hindrance? and how is a thing great or valuable which is naturally dead, or earth, or mud? Well then, do you possess nothing which is free? Perhaps nothing. And who is able to compel you to assent to that which appears false? No man. And who can compel you not to assent to that which appears true? No man. By this then you see that there is something in you naturally free. But to desire or to be averse from, or to move towards an object or to move from it, or to prepare yourself, or to propose to do anything, which of you can do this, unless he has received an impression of the appearance of that which is profitable or a duty? No man. You have then in these things also something which is not hindered and is free. Wretched men, work out this, take care of this, seek for good here.

THAT WE OUGHT NOT TO BE MOVED BY A DESIRE OF THOSE THINGS WHICH ARE NOT IN OUR POWER

Let not that which in another is contrary to nature be an evil to you; for you are not formed by nature to be depressed with others nor to be unhappy with others, but to be happy with them. If a man is unhappy, remember that his unhappiness is his own fault; for God has made all men to be happy, to be free from perturbations. For this purpose he has given means to them, some things to each person as his own, and other things not as his own; some things subject to hindrance and compulsion and deprivation; and these things are not a man's own; but the things which are not subject to hindrances, are his own; and the nature of good and evil, as it was fit to be done by him who takes care of us and protects us like a father, he has made our own. But you say, I have parted from a certain person, and he is grieved. Why did he consider as his own that which belongs to another? why, when he looked on you and was rejoiced, did he not also reckon that you are a mortal, that it is natural for you to part from him for a foreign country? Therefore he suffers the consequences of his own folly. But why do you or for what purpose bewail yourself? Is it that you also have not thought of these things? but like poor women who are good for nothing, you have enjoyed all things in which you took pleasure, as if you would always enjoy them, both places and men and conversation; and now you sit and weep because you do not see the same persons and do not live in the same places. Indeed you deserve this, to be more wretched than crows and ravens who have the power of flying where they please and changing their nests for others, and crossing the seas without lamenting or regretting their former condition. Yes, but this happens to them because they are irrational creatures. Was reason then given to us by the gods for the purpose of unhappiness and misery, that we may pass our lives in wretchedness and lamentation? Must all persons be immortal and must no man go abroad, and must we ourselves not go abroad, but remain rooted like plants; and if any of our familiar friends goes abroad, must we sit and weep; and on the contrary, when he returns, must we dance and clap our hands like children?

But my mother laments when she does not see me. Why has she not learned these principles? and I do not say this, that we should not take care that she may not lament, but I say that we ought not to desire in every way what is not our own. And the sorrow of another is another's sorrow; but my sorrow is my own. I then will stop my own sorrow by every means, for it is in my power; and the sorrow of another I will endeavor to stop as far as I can; but I will not attempt to do it by every means; for if I do, I shall be fighting against God, I shall be opposing Zeus and shall be placing myself against him in the administration of the universe; and the reward (the punishment) of this fighting against God and of this disobedience not only will the children of my children pay, but I also shall myself, both by day and by night, startled by dreams, perturbed, trembling at every piece of news, and having my tranquillity depending on the letters of others. Some person has arrived from Rome. I only hope there is no harm. But what harm can happen to you, where you are not? From Hellas (Greece) some one is come; I hope that there is no harm. In this way every place may be the cause of misfortune to you. Is it not enough for you to be unfortunate there where you are, and must you be so even beyond sea, and by the report of letters? Is this the way in which your affairs are in a state of security? Well then suppose that my friends have died in the places which are far from me. What else have they suffered than that which is the condition of mortals? Or how are you desirous at the same time to live to old age, and at the same time not to see the death of any person whom you love? Know you not that in the course of a long time many and various kinds of things must happen; that a fever shall overpower one, a robber another, and a third a tyrant? Such is the condition of things around us, such are those who live with us in the world; cold and heat, and unsuitable ways of living, and journeys by land, and voyages by sea, and winds, and various circumstances which surround us, destroy one man, and banish another, and throw one upon an embassy and another into an army. Sit down then in a flutter at all these things, lamenting, unhappy, unfortunate, dependent on another, and dependent not on one or two, but on ten thousands upon ten thousands.

Did you hear this when you were with the philosophers? did you learn this? do you not know that human life is a warfare? that one man must keep watch, another must go out as a spy, and a third must fight? and it is not possible that all should be in one place, nor is it better that it should be so. But you neglecting to do the commands of the general complain when anything more hard than usual is imposed on you, and you do not observe what you make the army become as far as it is in your power; that if all imitate you, no man will dig a trench, no man will put a rampart round, nor keep watch, nor expose himself to danger, but will appear to be useless for the purposes of an army. Again, in a vessel if you go as a sailor, keep to one place and stick to it. And if you are ordered to climb the mast, refuse; if to run to the head of the ship, refuse; and what master of a ship will endure you? and will he not pitch you overboard as a useless thing, an impediment only and bad example to the other sailors?

And so it is here also: every man's life is a kind of warfare, and it is long and diversified. You must observe the duty of a soldier and do every thing at the nod of the general; if it is possible, divining what his wishes are; for there is no resemblance between that general and this, neither in strength nor in superiority of character. Know you not that a good man does nothing for the sake of appearance, but for the sake of doing right? What advantage is it then to him to have done right? And what advantage is it to a man who writes the name of Dion to write it as he ought? The advantage is to have written it. Is there no reward then? Do you seek a reward for a good man greater than doing what is good and just? At Olympia you wish for nothing more, but it seems to you enough to be crowned at the games. Does it seem to you so small and worthless a thing to be good and happy? For these purposes being introduced by the gods into this city (the world), and it being now your duty to undertake the work of a man, do you still want nurses also and a mamma, and do foolish women by their weeping move you and make you effeminate? Will you thus never cease to be a foolish child? know you not that he who does the acts of a child, the older he is, the more ridiculous he is?

So in this matter also: if you kiss your own child, or your brother or friend, never give full license to the appearance (Greek: *phantasian*), and allow not your pleasure to go as far as it chooses; but check it, and curb it as those who stand behind men in their triumphs and remind them that they are mortal. Do you also remind yourself in like manner, that he whom you love is mortal, and that what you love is nothing of your own; it has been given to you for the present, not that it should not be taken from you, nor has it been given to you for all time, but as a fig is given to you or a bunch of grapes at the appointed season of the year. But if you wish for these things in winter, you are a fool. So if you wish for your son or friend when it is not allowed to you, you must know that you are wishing for a fig in winter. For such as winter is to a fig, such is every event which happens from the universe to the things which are taken away according to its nature. And further, at the times when you are delighted with a thing, place before yourself the contrary appearances. What harm is it while you are kissing your child to say with a lisping voice: To-morrow you will die; and to a friend also: To-morrow you will go away or I shall, and never shall we see one another again? But these are words of bad omen—and some incantations also are of bad omen; but because they are useful, I don't care for this; only let them be useful. But do you call things to be of bad omen except those which are significant of some evil? Cowardice is a word of bad omen, and meanness of spirit, and sorrow, and grief, and shamelessness. These words are of bad omen; and yet we ought not to hesitate to utter them in order to protect ourselves against the things. Do you tell me that a name which is significant of any natural thing is of evil omen? say that even for the ears of corn to be reaped is of bad omen, for it signifies the destruction of the ears, but not of the world. Say that the falling of the leaves also is of bad omen, and for the dried fig to take the place of the green fig, and for raisins to be made from the grapes. For all these things are changes from a former state into other states; not a destruction, but a certain fixed economy and administration. Such is going away from home and a small change: such is death, a greater change, not from the state which now is to that which is not, but to that which is not now. Shall I then no longer exist? You will not exist, but you will be something else, of which the world now has need; for you also came into existence not when you chose, but when the world had need of you.

Let these thoughts be ready to hand by night and by day; these you should write, these you should read; about these you should talk to yourself and to others. Ask a man: Can you help me at all for this purpose? and further, go to another and to another. Then if anything that is said be contrary to your wish, this reflection first will immediately relieve you, that it is not unexpected. For it is a great thing in all cases to say: I knew that I begot a son who is mortal. For so you also will say: I knew that I am mortal, I knew that I may leave my home, I knew that I may be ejected from it, I knew that I may be led to prison. Then if you turn round and look to yourself, and seek the place from which comes that which has happened, you will forthwith recollect that it comes from the place of things which are out of the power of the will, and of things which are not my own. What then is it to me? Then, you will ask, and this is the chief thing: And who is it that sent it? The leader, or the general, the state, the law of the state. Give it me then, for I must always obey the law in everything. Then, when the appearance (of things) pains you, for it is not in your power to prevent this, contend against it by the aid of reason, conquer it: do not allow it to gain strength nor to lead you to the consequences by raising images such as it pleases and as it pleases. If you be in Gyara, do not imagine the mode of living at Rome, and how many pleasures there were for him who lived there and how many there would be for him who returned to Rome; but fix your mind on this matter, how a man who lives in Gyara ought to live in Gyara like a man of courage. And if you be in Rome, do not imagine what the life in Athens is, but think only of the life in Rome.

Then in the place of all other delights substitute this, that of being conscious that you are obeying God, that not in word, but in deed you are performing the acts of a wise and good man. For what a thing it is for a man to be able to say to himself: Now whatever the rest may say in solemn manner in the schools and may be judged to be saying in a way contrary to common opinion (or in a strange way), this I am doing; and they are sitting and are discoursing of my virtues and inquiring about me and praising me; and of this Zeus has willed that I shall receive from myself a demonstration, and shall myself know if he has a soldier such as he ought to have, a citizen such as he ought to have, and if he has chosen to produce me to the rest of mankind as a witness of the things which are independent of the will: See that you fear without reason, that you foolishly desire what you do desire; seek not the good in things external; seek it in yourselves: if you do not, you will not find it. For this purpose he leads me at one time hither, at another time sends me thither, shows me to men as poor, without authority, and sick; sends me to Gyara, leads me into prison, not because he hates me—far from him be such a meaning, for who hates the best of his servants? nor yet because he cares not for me, for he does not neglect any even of the smallest things; but he does this for the purpose of exercising me and making use of me as a witness to others. Being appointed to such a service, do I still care about the place in which I am, or with whom I am, or what men say about me? and do I not entirely direct my thoughts to God and to his instructions and commands?

Having these things (or thoughts) always in hand, and exercising them by yourself, and keeping them in readiness, you will never be in want of one to comfort you and strengthen you. For it is not shameful to be without something to eat, but not to have reason sufficient for keeping away fear and sorrow. But if once you have gained exemption from sorrow and fear, will there any longer be a tyrant for you, or a tyrant's guard, or attendants on Caesar? Or shall any appointment to offices at court cause you pain, or shall those who sacrifice in the Capitol on the occasion of being named to certain functions, cause pain to you who have received so great authority from Zeus? Only do not make a proud display of it, nor boast of it; but show it by your acts; and if no man perceives it, be satisfied that you are yourself in a healthy state and happy.

TO THOSE WHO FALL OFF (DESIST) FROM THEIR PURPOSE

Consider as to the things which you proposed to yourself at first, which you have secured, and which you have not; and how you are pleased when you recall to memory the one, and are pained about the other; and if it is possible, recover the things wherein you failed. For we must not shrink when we are engaged in the greatest combat, but we must even take blows. For the combat before us is not in wrestling and the Pancration, in which both the successful and the unsuccessful may have the greatest merit, or may have little, and in truth may be very fortunate or very unfortunate; but the combat is for good fortune and happiness themselves. Well then, even if we have renounced the contest in this matter (for good fortune and happiness), no man hinders us from renewing the combat again, and we are not compelled to wait for another four years that the games at Olympia may come again; but as soon as you have recovered and restored yourself, and employ the same zeal, you may renew the combat again; and if again you renounce it, you may again renew it; and if you once gain the victory, you are like him who has never renounced the combat.

Only do not through a habit of doing the same thing (renouncing the combat), begin to do it with pleasure, and then like a bad athlete go about after being conquered in all the circuit of the games like quails who have run away.

TO THOSE WHO FEAR WANT

Are you not ashamed at being more cowardly and more mean than fugitive slaves? How do they when they run away leave their masters? on what estates do they depend, and what domestics do they rely on? Do they not after stealing a little, which is enough for the first days, then afterwards move on through land or through sea, contriving one method after another for maintaining their lives? And what fugitive slave ever died of hunger? But you are afraid lest necessary things should fail you, and are sleepless by night. Wretch, are you so blind, and don't you see the road to which the want of necessaries leads?—Well, where does it lead?—to the same place to which a fever leads, or a stone that falls on you, to death. Have you not often said this yourself to your companions? have you not read much of this kind, and written much? and how often have you boasted that you were easy as to death?

Learn then first what are the things which are shameful, and then tell us that you are a philosopher: but at present do not, even if any other man calls you so, allow it.

Is that shameful to you which is not your own act, that of which you are not the cause, that which has come to you by accident, as a headache, as a fever? If your parents were poor, and left their property to others, and if while they live, they do not help you at all, is this shameful to you? Is this what you learned with the philosophers? Did you never hear that the thing which is shameful ought to be blamed, and that which is blamable is worthy of blame? Whom do you blame for an act which is not his own, which he did not do himself? Did you then make your father such as he is, or is it in your power to improve him? Is this power given to you? Well then, ought you to wish the things which are not given to you, or to be ashamed if you do not obtain them? And have you also been accustomed while you were studying philosophy to look to others and to hope for nothing from yourself? Lament then and groan and eat with fear that you may not have food to-morrow. Tremble about your poor slaves lest they steal, lest they run away, lest they die. So live, and continue to live, you who in name only have approached philosophy, and have disgraced its theorems as far as you can by showing them to be useless and unprofitable to those who take them up; you, who have never sought constancy, freedom from perturbation, and from passions; you who have not sought any person for the sake of this object, but many for the sake of syllogisms; you who have never thoroughly examined any of these appearances by yourself, Am I able to bear, or am I not able to bear? What remains for me to do? But as if all your affairs were well and secure, you have been resting on the third topic, that of things being unchanged, in order that you may possess unchanged—what? cowardice, mean spirit, the admiration of the rich, desire without attaining any end, and avoidance (Greek: *echchlisin*) which fails in the attempt? About security in these things you have been anxious.

Ought you not to have gained something in addition from reason, and then to have protected this with security? And whom did you ever see building a battlement all around and encircling it with a wall? And what doorkeeper is placed with no door to watch? But you practise in order to be able to prove—what? You practise that you may not be tossed as on the sea through sophisms, and tossed about from what? Show me first what you hold, what you measure, or what you weigh; and show me the scales or the medimnus (the measure); or how long will you go on measuring the dust? Ought you not to demonstrate those things which make men happy, which make things go on for them in the way as they wish, and why we ought to blame no man, accuse no man, and acquiesce in the administration of the universe?

ABOUT FREEDOM

He is free who lives as he wishes to live; who is neither subject to compulsion nor to hindrance, nor to force; whose movements to action (Greek: *hormai*) are not impeded, whose desires attain their purpose, and who does not fall into that which he would avoid (Greek: *echchliseis aperiptotoi*). Who then chooses to live in error? No man. Who chooses to live deceived, liable to mistake, unjust, unrestrained, discontented, mean? No man. Not one then of the bad lives as he wishes; nor is he then free. And who chooses to live in sorrow, fear, envy, pity, desiring and failing in his desires, attempting to avoid something and falling into it? Not one. Do we then find any of the bad free from sorrow, free from fear, who does not fall into that which he would avoid, and does not obtain that which he wishes? Not one; nor then do we find any bad man free.

Further, then, answer me this question, also: does freedom seem to you to be something great and noble and valuable? How should it not seem so? Is it possible then when a man obtains anything so great and valuable and noble to be mean? It is not possible. When then you see any man subject to another or flattering him contrary to his own opinion, confidently affirm that this man also is not free; and not only if he do this for a bit of supper, but also if he does it for a government (province) or a consulship; and call these men little slaves who for the sake of little matters do these things, and those who do so for the sake of great things call great slaves, as they deserve to be. This is admitted also. Do you think that freedom is a thing independent and self-governing? Certainly. Whomsoever then it is in the power of another to hinder and compel, declare that he is not free. And do not look, I entreat you, after his grandfathers and great-grandfathers, or inquire about his being bought or sold, but if you hear him saying from his heart and with feeling, "Master," even if the twelve fasces precede him (as consul), call him a slave. And if you hear him say, "Wretch that I am, how much I suffer," call him a slave. If, finally, you see him lamenting, complaining, unhappy, call him a slave, though he wears a praetexta. If, then, he is doing nothing of this kind do not yet say that he is free, but learn his opinions, whether they are subject to compulsion, or may produce hindrance, or to bad fortune, and if you find him such, call him a slave who has a holiday in the Saturnalia; say that his master is from home; he will return soon, and you will know what he suffers.

What then is that which makes a man free from hindrance and makes him his own master? For wealth does not do it, nor consulship, nor provincial government, nor royal power; but something else must be discovered. What then is that which when we write makes us free from hindrance and unimpeded? The knowledge of the art of writing. What then is it in playing the lute? The science of playing the lute. Therefore in life also it is the science of life. You have then heard in a general way; but examine the thing also in the several parts. Is it possible that he who desires any of the things which depend on others can be free from hindrance? No. Is it possible for him to be unimpeded? No. Therefore he cannot be free. Consider then, whether we have nothing which is in our own power only, or whether we have all things, or whether some things are in our own power, and others in the power of others. What do you mean? When you wish the body to be entire (sound) is it in your power or not? It is not in my power. When you wish it to be healthy? Neither is this in my power. When you wish it to be handsome? Nor is this. Life or death? Neither is this in my power. Your body then is another's, subject to every man who is stronger than yourself. It is. But your estate is it in your power to have it when you please, and as long as you please, and such as you please? No. And your slaves? No. And your clothes? No. And your house? No. And your horses? Not one of these things. And if you wish by all means your children to live, or your wife, or your brother, or your friends, is it in your power? This also is not in my power.

Whether then have you nothing which is in your own power, which depends on yourself only and cannot be taken from you, or have you anything of the kind? I know not. Look at the thing then thus, and examine it. Is any man able to make you assent to that which is false? No man. In the matter of assent then you are free from hindrance and obstruction. Granted. Well; and can a man force you to desire to move towards that to which you do not choose? He can, for when he threatens me with death or bonds he compels me to desire to move towards it. If then you despise death and bonds, do you still pay any regard to him? No. Is then the despising of death an act of your own or is it not yours? It is my act.

When you have made this preparation, and have practised this discipline, to distinguish that which belongs to another from that which is your own, the things which are subject to hindrance from those which are not, to consider the things free from hindrance to concern yourself, and those which are not free not to concern yourself, to keep your desire steadily fixed to the things which do concern yourself, and turned from the things which do not concern yourself; do you still fear any man? No one. For about what will you be afraid? About the things which are your own, in which consists the nature of good and evil? and who has power over these things? who can take them away? who can impede them? No man can, no more than he can impede God. But will you be afraid about your body and your possessions, about things which are not yours, about things which in no way concern you? and what else have you been studying from the beginning than to distinguish between your own and not your own, the things which are in your power and not in your power, the things subject to hindrance and not subject? and why have you come to the philosophers? was it that you may nevertheless be unfortunate and unhappy? You will then in this way, as I have supposed you to have done, be without fear and disturbance. And what is grief to you? for fear comes from what you expect, but grief from that which is present. But what further will you desire? For of the things which are within the power of the will, as being good and present, you have a proper and regulated desire; but of the things which are not in the power of the will you do not desire any one, and so you do not allow any place to that which is irrational, and impatient, and above measure hasty.

Then after receiving everything from another and even yourself, are you angry and do you blame the giver if he takes anything from you? Who are you, and for what purpose did you come into the world? Did not he (God) introduce you here, did he not show you the light, did he not give you fellow-workers, and perceptions and reason? and as whom did he introduce you here? did he not introduce you as subject to death, and as one to live on the earth with a little flesh, and to observe his administration, and to join with him in the spectacle and the festival for a short time? Will you not then, as long as you have been permitted, after seeing the spectacle and the solemnity, when he leads you out, go with adoration of him and thanks for what you have heard and seen? No; but I would still enjoy the feast. The initiated too would wish to be longer in the initiation; and perhaps also those at Olympia to see other athletes. But the solemnity is ended; go away like a grateful and modest man; make room for others; others also must be born, as you were, and, being born, they must have a place, and houses, and necessary things. And if the first do not retire, what remains? Why are you insatiable? Why are you not content? why do you contract the world? Yes, but I would have my little children with me and my wife. What, are they yours? do they not belong to the giver, and to him who made you? then will you not give up what belongs to others? will you not give way to him who is superior? Why then did he introduce me into the world on these conditions? And if the conditions do not suit you, depart. He has no need of a spectator who is not satisfied. He wants those who join in the festival, those who take part in the chorus, that they may rather applaud, admire, and celebrate with hymns the solemnity. But those who can bear no trouble, and the cowardly, he will not unwillingly see absent from the great assembly (Greek: *panaeguris*) for they did not when they were present behave as they ought to do at a festival nor fill up their place properly, but they lamented, found fault with the deity, fortune, their companions; not seeing both what they had, and their own powers, which they received for contrary purposes, the powers of magnanimity, of a generous mind, manly spirit, and what we are now inquiring about, freedom. For what purpose then have I received these things? To use them. How long? So long as he who has lent them chooses. What if they are necessary to me? Do not attach yourself to them and they will not be necessary; do not say to yourself that they are necessary, and then they are not necessary.

You then, a man may say, are you free? I wish, by the gods, and pray to be free; but I am not yet able to face my masters, I still value my poor body, I value greatly the preservation of it entire, though I do not possess it entire. But I can point out to you a free man, that you may no longer seek an example. Diogenes was free. How was he free? Not because he was born of free parents, but because he was himself free, because he had cast off all the handles of slavery, and it was not possible for any man to approach him, nor had any man the means of laying hold of him to enslave him. He had everything easily loosed, everything only hanging to him. If you laid hold of his property, he would have rather let it go and be yours, than he would have followed you for it; if you had laid hold of his leg, he would have let go his leg; if of all his body, all his poor body; his intimates, friends, country, just the same. For he knew from whence he had them, and from whom, and on what conditions. His true parents indeed, the gods, and his real country he would never have deserted, nor would he have yielded to any man in obedience to them and to their orders, nor would any man have died for his country more readily. For he was not used to inquire when he should be considered to have done anything on behalf of the whole of things (the universe, or all the world), but he remembered that everything which is done comes from thence and is done on behalf of that country and is commanded by him who administers it. Therefore see what Diogenes himself says and writes: "For this reason," he says, "Diogenes, it is in your power to speak both with the King of the Persians and with Archidamus the King of the Lacedaemonians, as you please." Was it because he was born of free parents? I suppose all the Athenians and all the Lacedaemonians, because they were born of slaves, could not talk with them (these kings) as they wished, but feared and paid court to them. Why then does he say that it is in his power? Because I do not consider the poor body to be my own, because I want nothing, because law is everything to me, and nothing else is. These were the things which permitted him to be free.

Think of these things, these opinions, these words; look to these examples, if you would be free, if you desire the thing according to its worth. And what is the wonder if you buy so great a thing at the price of things so many and so great? For the sake of this which is called liberty, some hang themselves, others throw themselves down precipices, and sometimes even whole cities have perished; and will you not for the sake of the true and unassailable and secure liberty give back to God when he demands them the things which he has given? Will you not, as Plato says, study not to die only, but also to endure torture, and exile, and scourging, and, in a word, to give up all which is not your own? If you will not, you will be a slave among slaves, even if you be ten thousand times a consul; and if you make your way up to the palace (Caesar's residence), you will no less be a slave; and you will feel that perhaps philosophers utter words which are contrary to common opinion (paradoxes), as Cleanthes also said, but not words contrary to reason. For you will know by experience that the words are true, and that there is no profit from the things which are valued and eagerly sought to those who have obtained them; and to those who have not yet obtained them there is an imagination (Greek: *phantasia*), that when these things are come, all that is good will come with them; then, when they are come, the feverish feeling is the same, the tossing to and fro is the same, the satiety, the desire of things, which are not present; for freedom is acquired not by the full possession of the things which are desired, but by removing the desire. And that you may know that this is true, as you have labored for those things, so transfer your labor to these: be vigilant for the purpose of acquiring an opinion which will make you free; pay court to a philosopher instead of to a rich old man; be seen about a philosopher's doors; you will not disgrace yourself by being seen; you will not go away empty nor without profit, if you go to the philosopher as you ought, and if not (if you do not succeed), try at least; the trial (attempt) is not disgraceful.

ON FAMILIAR INTIMACY

To this matter before all you must attend, that you be never so closely connected with any of your former intimates or friends as to come down to the same acts as he does. If you do not observe this rule, you will ruin yourself. But if the thought arises in your mind, "I shall seem disobliging to him and he will not have the same feeling towards me," remember that nothing is done without cost, nor is it possible for a man if he does not do the same things to be the same man that he was. Choose then which of the two you will have, to be equally loved by those by whom you were formerly loved, being the same with your former self; or, being superior, not to obtain from your friends the same that you did before.

WHAT THINGS WE SHOULD EXCHANGE FOR OTHER THINGS

Keep this thought in readiness, when you lose anything external, what you acquire in place of it; and if it be worth more, never say, I have had a loss; neither if you have got a horse in place of an ass, or an ox in place of a sheep, nor a good action in place of a bit of money, nor in place of idle talk such tranquillity as befits a man, nor in place of lewd talk if you have acquired modesty. If you remember this, you will always maintain your character such as it ought to be. But if you do not, consider that the times of opportunity are perishing, and that whatever pains you take about yourself, you are going to waste them all and overturn them. And it needs only a few things for the loss and overturning of all—namely, a small deviation from reason. For the steerer of a ship to upset it, he has no need of the same means as he has need of for saving it; but if he turns it a little to the wind, it is lost; and if he does not do this purposely, but has been neglecting his duty a little, the ship is lost. Something of the kind happens in this case also; if you only fall a nodding a little, all that you have up to this time collected is gone. Attend therefore to the ap that which you have tes of things, and watch over them; for and fidelity and constancye is no small matter, but it is modesty undisturbed, freedom from dom from the affects, a state of mind what will you sell these thing tranquillity, in a word liberty. For which you will obtain in exchan what is the value of the things any such thing for it?—See, and these.—But shall I not obtain what you receive in place of it. I p u do in return get that, see tribuneship: he possesses a praetorship, ss decency, he possesses a not make acclamations where it is not be ossess modesty. But I do where I ought not; for I am free, and a frien ing: I will not stand up him willingly. But I must not claim (seek) anything f God. and so I obey nor possession, nor magistracy, nor good report, nor se, neither body For he (God) does not allow me to claim (seek) them, fact anything. chosen, he would have made them good for me; but he has not done so, and for this reason I cannot transgress his commands. Preserve that which is your own good in everything; and as to every other thing, as it is permitted, and so far as to behave consistently with reason in respect to them, content with this only. If you do not, you will be unfortunate, you will fail in all things, you will be hindered, you will be impeded. These are the laws which have been sent from thence (from God); these are the orders. Of these laws a man ought to be an expositor, to these he ought to submit, not to those of Masurius and Cassius.

TO THOSE WHO ARE DESIROUS OF PASSING LIFE IN TRANQUILLITY

Remember that not only the desire of power and of riches makes us mean and subject to others, but even the desire of tranquillity, and of leisure, and of travelling abroad, and of learning. For, to speak plainly, whatever the external thing may be, the value which we set upon it places us in subjection to others. What then is the difference between desiring to be a senator or not desiring to be one; what is the difference between desiring power or being content with a private station; what is the difference between saying, I am unhappy, I have nothing to do, but I am bound to my books as a corpse; or saying, I am unhappy, I have no leisure for reading? For as salutations and power are things external and independent of the will, so is a book. For what purpose do you choose to read? Tell me. For if you only direct your purpose to being amused or learning something, you are a silly fellow and incapable of enduring labor. But if you refer reading to the proper end, what else is this than a tranquil and happy life (Greek: *eusoia*)? But if reading does not secure for you a happy and tranquil life, what is the use of it? But it does secure this, the man replies, and for this reason I am vexed that I am deprived of it.—And what is this tranquil and happy life, which any man can impede, I do not say Caesar or Caesar's friend, but a crow, a piper, a fever, and thirty thousand other things? But a tranquil and happy life contains nothing so sure as continuity and freedom from obstacle. Now I am called to do something: I will go then with the purpose of observing the measures (rules) which I must keep, of acting with modesty, steadiness, without desire and aversion to things external; and then that I may attend to men, what they say, how they are moved; and this not with any bad disposition, or that I may have something to blame or to ridicule; but I turn to myself, and ask if I also commit the same faults. How then shall I cease to commit them? Formerly I also acted wrong, but now I do not: thanks to God.

What then is the reason of this? The reason is that we have never read for this purpose, we have never written for this purpose, so that we may in our actions use in a way conformable to nature the appearances presented to us; but we terminate in this, in learning what is said, and in being able to expound it to another, in resolving a syllogism, and in handling the hypothetical syllogism. For this reason where our study (purpose) is, there alone is the impediment. Would you have by all means the things which are not in your power? Be prevented then, be hindered, fail in your purpose. But if we read what is written about action (efforts, Greek: *hormae*), not that we may see what is said about action, but that we may act well; if we read what is said about desire and aversion (avoiding things), in order that we may neither fail in our desires, nor fall into that which we try to avoid; if we read what is said about duty (officium), in order that remembering the relations (of things to one another) we may do nothing irrationally nor contrary to these relations; we should not be vexed, in being hindered as to our readings, but we should be satisfied with doing the acts which are conformable (to the relations), and we should be reckoning not what so far we have been accustomed to reckon: To-day I have read so many verses, I have written so many; but (we should say), To-day I have employed my action as it is taught by the philosophers; I have not employed my desire; I have used avoidance (Greek: *echchlisei*) only with respect to things which are within the power of my will; I have not been afraid of such a person, I have not been prevailed upon by the entreaties of another; I have exercised my patience, my abstinence, my co-operation with others; and so we should thank God for what we ought to thank him.

There is only one way to happiness, and let this rule be ready both in the morning and during the day and by night: the rule is not to look towards things which are out of the power of our will, to think that nothing is our own, to give up all things to the Divinity, to Fortune; to make them the superintendents of these things, whom Zeus also has made so; for a man to observe that only which is his own, that which cannot be hindered; and when we read, to refer our reading to this only, and our writing and our listening. For this reason I cannot call the man industrious, if I hear this only, that he reads and writes; and even if a man adds that he reads all night, I cannot say so, if he knows not to what he should refer his reading. For neither do you say that a man is industrious if he keeps awake for a girl, nor do I. But if he does it (reads and writes) for reputation, I say that he is a lover of reputation. And if he does it for money, I say that he is a lover of money, not a lover of labor; and if he does it through love of learning, I say that he is a lover of learning. But if he refers his labor to his own ruling power that he may keep it in a state conformable to nature and pass his life in that state, then only do I say that he is industrious. For never commend a man on account of these things which are common to all, but on account of his opinions (principles); for these are the things which belong to each man, which make his actions bad or good. Remembering these rules, rejoice in that which is present, and be content with the things which come in season. If you see anything which you have learned and inquired about occurring to you in your course of life (or opportunely applied by you to the acts of life), be delighted at it.

If you have laid aside or have lessened bad disposition and a habit of reviling; if you have done so with rash temper, obscene words, hastiness, sluggishness; if you are not moved by what you formerly were, and not in the same way as you once were, you can celebrate a festival daily, to-day because you have behaved well in one act, and to-morrow because you have behaved well in another. How much greater is this a reason for making sacrifices than a consulship or the government of a province? These things come to you from yourself and from the gods. Remember this, who gives these things and to whom, and for what purpose. If you cherish yourself in these thoughts, do you still think that it makes any difference where you shall be happy, where you shall please God? Are not the gods equally distant from all places? Do they not see from all places alike that which is going on?

AGAINST THE QUARRELSOME AND FEROCIOUS

The wise and good man neither himself fights with any person, nor does he allow another, so far as he can prevent it. And an example of this as well as of all other things is proposed to us in the life of Socrates, who not only himself on all occasions avoided fights (quarrels), but would not allow even others to quarrel. See in Xenophon's Symposium how many quarrels he settled, how further he endured Thrasymachus and Polus and Callicles; how he tolerated his wife, and how he tolerated his son who attempted to confute him and to cavil with him. For he remembered well that no man has in his power another man's ruling principle. He wished therefore for nothing else than that which was his own. And what is this? Not that this or that man may act according to nature, for that is a thing which belongs to another; but that while others are doing their own acts, as they choose, he may nevertheless be in a condition conformable to nature and live in it, only doing what is his own to the end that others also may be in a state conformable to nature. For this is the object always set before him by the wise and good man. Is it to be commander (a praetor) of an army? No; but if it is permitted him, his object is in this matter to maintain his own ruling principle. Is it to marry? No; but if marriage is allowed to him, in this matter his object is to maintain himself in a condition conformable to nature. But if he would have his son not to do wrong or his wife, he would have what belongs to another not to belong to another: and to be instructed is this, to learn what things are a man's own and what belongs to another.

How then is there left any place for fighting (quarrelling) to a man who has this opinion (which he ought to have)? Is he surprised at any thing which happens, and does it appear new to him? Does he not expect that which comes from the bad to be worse and more grievous than that what actually befalls him? And does he not reckon as pure gain whatever they (the bad) may do which falls short of extreme wickedness? Such a person has reviled you. Great thanks to him for not having struck you. But he has struck me also. Great thanks that he did not wound you. But he wounded me also. Great thanks that he did not kill you. For when did he learn or in what school that man is a tame animal, that men love one another, that an act of injustice is a great harm to him who does it. Since then he has not learned this and is not convinced of it, why shall he not follow that which seems to be for his own interest? Your neighbor has thrown stones. Have you then done anything wrong? But the things in the house have been broken. Are you then a utensil? No; but a free power of will. What then is given to you (to do) in answer to this? If you are like a wolf, you must bite in return, and throw more stones. But, if you consider what is proper for a man, examine your storehouse, see with what faculties you came into the world. Have you the disposition of a wild beast, have you the disposition of revenge for an injury? When is a horse wretched? When he is deprived of his natural faculties, not when he cannot crow like a cock, but when he cannot run. When is a dog wretched? Not when he cannot fly, but when he cannot track his game. Is then a man also unhappy in this way, not because he cannot strangle lions or embrace statues, for he did not come into the world in the possession of certain powers from nature for this purpose, but because he has lost his probity and his fidelity? People ought to meet and lament such a man for the misfortunes into which he has fallen; not indeed to lament because a man has been born or has died, but because it has happened to him in his lifetime to have lost the things which are his own, not that which he received from his father, not his land and house, and his inn, and his slaves; for not one of these things is a man's own, but all belong to others, are servile, and subject to account (Greek: *hupeithuna*), at different times given to different persons by those who have them in their power: but I mean the things which belong to him as a man, the marks (stamps) in his mind with which he came into the world, such as we seek also on coins, and if we find them we approve of the coins, and if we do not find the marks we reject them. What is the stamp on this sestertius? The stamp of Trajan. Present it. It is the stamp of Nero. Throw it away; it cannot be accepted, it is counterfeit. So also in this case: What is the stamp of his opinions? It is gentleness, a sociable disposition, a tolerant temper, a disposition to mutual affections. Produce these qualities. I accept them: I consider this man a citizen, I accept him as a neighbor, a companion in my voyages. Only see that he has not Nero's stamp. Is he passionate, is he full of resentment, is he fault-finding? If the whim seizes him, does he break the heads of those who come in his way? (If so), why then did you say that he is a man? Is everything judged (determined) by the bare form? If that is so, say that the form in wax is an apple and has the smell and the taste of an apple. But the external figure is not enough: neither then is the nose enough and the eyes to make the man, but he must have the opinions of a man. Here is a man who does not listen to reason, who does not know when he is refuted: he is an ass; in another man the sense of shame is become dead: he is good for nothing, he is anything rather than a man. This man seeks whom he may meet and kick or bite, so that he is not even a sheep or an ass, but a kind of wild beast.

What then? would you have me to be despised?—By whom? by those who know you? and how shall those who know you despise a man who is gentle and modest? Perhaps you mean by those who do not know you? What is that to you? For no other artisan cares for the opinion of those who know not his art. But they will be more hostile to me for this reason. Why do you say "me"? Can any man injure your will, or prevent you from using in a natural way the appearances which are presented to you? In no way can he. Why then are you still disturbed and why do you choose to show yourself afraid? And why do you not come forth and proclaim that you are at peace with all men whatever they may do, and laugh at those chiefly who think that they can harm you? These slaves, you can say, know not either who I am, nor where lies my good or my evil, because they have no access to the things which are mine.

In this way also those who occupy a strong city mock the besiegers (and say): What trouble these men are now taking for nothing; our wall is secure, we have food for a very long time, and all other resources. These are the things which make a city strong and impregnable; but nothing else than his opinions makes a man's soul impregnable. For what wall is so strong, or what body is so hard, or what possession is so safe, or what honor (rank, character) so free from assault (as a man's opinions)? All (other) things everywhere are perishable, easily taken by assault, and if any man in any way is attached to them, he must be disturbed, except what is bad, he must fear, lament, find his desires disappointed, and fall into things which he would avoid. Then do we not choose to make secure the only means of safety which are offered to us, and do we not choose to withdraw ourselves from that which is perishable and servile and to labor at the things which are imperishable and by nature free; and do we not remember that no man either hurts another or does good to another, but that a man's opinions about each thing, is that which hurts him, is that which overturns him; this is fighting, this is civil discord, this is war? That which made Eteocles and Polynices enemies was nothing else than this opinion which they had about royal power, their opinion about exile, that the one is the extreme of evils, the other the greatest good. Now this is the nature of every man to seek the good, to avoid the bad; to consider him who deprives us of the one and involves us in the other an enemy and treacherous, even if he be a brother, or a son, or a father. For nothing is more akin to us than the good; therefore, if these things (externals) are good and evil, neither is a father a friend to sons, nor a brother to a brother, but all the world is everywhere full of enemies, treacherous men, and sycophants. But if the will (Greek: *proairesis*, the purpose, the intention) being what it ought to be, is the only good; and if the will being such as it ought not to be, is the only evil, where is there any strife, where is there reviling? about what? about the things which do not concern us? and strife with whom? with the ignorant, the unhappy, with those who are deceived about the chief things?

Remembering this Socrates managed his own house and endured a very ill-tempered wife and a foolish (ungrateful?) son.

AGAINST THOSE WHO LAMENT OVER BEING PITIED

I am grieved, a man says, at being pitied. Whether then is the fact of your being pitied a thing which concerns you or those who pity you? Well, is it in your power to stop this pity? It is in my power, if I show them that I do not require pity. And whether then are you in the condition of not deserving (requiring) pity, or are you not in that condition? I think that I am not; but these persons do not pity me, for the things for which, if they ought to pity me, it would be proper, I mean, for my faults; but they pity me for my poverty, for not possessing honorable offices, for diseases and deaths and other such things. Whether then are you prepared to convince the many, that not one of these things is an evil, but that it is possible for a man who is poor and has no office (Greek: *anarchonti*) and enjoys no honor to be happy; or to show yourself to them as rich and in power? For the second of these things belong to a man who is boastful, silly, and good for nothing. And consider by what means the pretence must be supported. It will be necessary for you to hire slaves and to possess a few silver vessels, and to exhibit them in public, if it is possible, though they are often the same, and to attempt to conceal the fact that they are the same, and to have splendid garments, and all other things for display, and to show that you are a man honored by the great, and to try to sup at their houses, or to be supposed to sup there, and as to your person to employ some mean arts, that you may appear to be more handsome and nobler than you are. These things you must contrive, if you choose to go by the second path in order not to be pitied. But the first way is both impracticable and long, to attempt the very thing which Zeus has not been able to do, to convince all men what things are good and bad. Is this power given to you? This only is given to you, to convince yourself; and you have not convinced yourself. Then I ask you, do you attempt to persuade other men? and who has lived so long with you as you with yourself? and who has so much power of convincing you as you have of convincing yourself; and who is better disposed and nearer to you than you are to yourself? How then have you not yet convinced yourself in order to learn? At present are not things upside down? Is this what you have been earnest about doing, to learn to be free from grief and free from disturbance, and not to be humbled (abject), and to be free? Have you not heard then that there is only one way which leads to this end, to give up (dismiss) the things which do not depend on the will, to withdraw from them, and to admit that they belong to others? For another man then to have an opinion about you, of what kind is it? It is a thing independent of the will—Then is it nothing to you? It is nothing. When then you are still vexed at this and disturbed, do you think that you are convinced about good and evil?

ON FREEDOM FROM FEAR

What makes the tyrant formidable? The guards, you say, and their swords, and the men of the bedchamber, and those who exclude them who would enter. Why then if you bring a boy (child) to the tyrant when he is with his guards, is he not afraid; or is it because the child does not understand these things? If then any man does understand what guards are and that they have swords, and comes to the tyrant for this very purpose because he wishes to die on account of some circumstance and seeks to die easily by the hand of another, is he afraid of the guards? No, for he wishes for the thing which makes the guards formidable. If then any man neither wishing to die nor to live by all means, but only as it may be permitted, approaches the tyrant what hinders him from approaching the tyrant without fear? Nothing. If then a man has the same opinion about his property as the man whom I have instanced has about his body; and also about his children and his wife, and in a word is so affected by some madness or despair that he cares not whether he possesses them or not, but like children who are playing with shells (quarrel) about the play, but do not trouble themselves about the shells, so he too has set no value on the materials (things), but values the pleasure that he has with them and the occupation, what tyrant is then formidable to him, or what guards or what swords?

What hinders a man, who has clearly separated (comprehended) these things, from living with a light heart and bearing easily the reins, quietly expecting everything which can happen, and enduring that which has already happened? Would you have me to bear poverty? Come and you will know what poverty is when it has found one who can act well the part of a poor man. Would you have me to possess power? Let me have power, and also the trouble of it. Well, banishment? Wherever I shall go, there it will be well with me; for here also where I am, it was not because of the place that it was well with me, but because of my opinions which I shall carry off with me, for neither can any man deprive me of them; but my opinions alone are mine and they cannot be taken from me, and I am satisfied while I have them, wherever I may be and whatever I am doing. But now it is time to die. Why do you say to die? Make no tragedy show of the thing, but speak of it as it is. It is now time for the matter (of the body) to be resolved into the things out of which it was composed. And what is the formidable thing here? what is going to perish of the things which are in the universe? what new thing or wondrous is going to happen? Is it for this reason that a tyrant is formidable? Is it for this reason that the guards appear to have swords which are large and sharp? Say this to others; but I have considered about all these things; no man has power over me. I have been made free; I know his commands, no man can now lead me as a slave. I have a proper person to assert my freedom; I have proper judges. (I say) are you not the master of my body? What then is that to me? Are you not the master of my property? What then is that to me? Are you not the master of my exile or of my chains? Well, from all these things and all the poor body itself I depart at your bidding, when you please. Make trial of your power, and you will know how far it reaches.

Whom then can I still fear? Those who are over the bedchamber? Lest they should do, what? Shut me out? If they find that I wish to enter, let them shut me out. Why then do you go to the doors? Because I think it befits me, while the play (sport) lasts, to join in it. How then are you not shut out? Because unless some one allows me to go in, I do not choose to go in, but am always content with that which happens; for I think that what God chooses is better than what I choose. I will attach myself as a minister and follower to him; I have the same movements (pursuits) as he has, I have the same desires; in a word, I have the same will (Greek: *sunthelo*). There is no shutting out for me, but for those who would force their way in. Why then do not I force my way in? Because I know that nothing good is distributed within to those who enter. But when I hear any man called fortunate because he is honored by Caesar, I say what does he happen to get? A province (the government of a province). Does he also obtain an opinion such as he ought? The office of a Prefect. Does he also obtain the power of using his office well? Why do I still strive to enter (Caesar's chamber)? A man scatters dried figs and nuts: the children seize them, and fight with one another; men do not, for they think them to be a small matter. But if a man should throw about shells, even the children do not seize them. Provinces are distributed: let children look to that. Money is distributed; let children look to that. Praetorships, consulships, are distributed; let children scramble for them, let them be shut out, beaten, kiss the hands of the giver, of the slaves: but to me these are only dried figs and nuts. What then? If you fail to get them, while Caesar is scattering them about, do not be troubled; if a dried fig come into your lap, take it and eat it; for so far you may value even a fig. But if I shall stoop down and turn another over, or be turned over by another, and shall flatter those who have got into (Caesar's) chamber, neither is a dried fig worth the trouble, nor anything else of the things which are not good, which the philosophers have persuaded me not to think good.

TO A PERSON WHO HAD BEEN CHANGED TO A CHARACTER OF SHAMELESSNESS

When you see another man in the possession of power (magistracy), set against this the fact that you have not the want (desire) of power; when you see another rich, see what you possess in place of riches: for if you possess nothing in place of them, you are miserable; but if you have not the want of riches, know that you possess more than this man possesses and what is worth much more.

WHAT THINGS WE OUGHT TO DESPISE AND WHAT THINGS WE OUGHT TO VALUE

The difficulties of all men are about external things, their helplessness is about external. What shall I do? how will it be? how will it turn out? will this happen? will that? All these are the words of those who are turning themselves to things which are not within the power of the will. For who says, How shall I not assent to that which is false? how shall I not turn away from the truth? If a man be of such a good disposition as to be anxious about these things I will remind him of this: Why are you anxious? The thing is in your own power, be assured; do not be precipitate in assenting before you apply the natural rule. On the other side, if a man is anxious (uneasy) about desire, lest it fail in its purpose and miss its end, and with respect to the avoidance of things, lest he should fall into that which he would avoid, I will first kiss (love) him, because he throws away the things about which others are in a flutter (others desire) and their fears, and employs his thoughts about his own affairs and his own condition. Then I shall say to him: If you do not choose to desire that which you will fail to obt[illegible] to attempt to avoid that into which you will fall, desire nothing which belongs to (which is in the power of) others, nor try to avoid any of the things which are not in your power. If you do not observe this rule, you must of necessity fail in your desires and fall into that which you would avoid. What is the difficulty here? where is the room for the words How will it be? and How will it turn out? and Will this happen or that?

Now is not that which will happen independent of the will? Yes. And the nature of good and of evil, is it not in the things which are within the power of the will? Yes. Is it in your power then to treat according to nature everything which happens? Can any person hinder you? No man. No longer then say to me, How will it be? For, however it may be, you will dispose of it well, and the result to you will be a fortunate one. What would Hercules have been if he said: How shall a great lion not appear to me, or a great boar, or savage men? And what do you care for that? If a great boar appear, you will fight a greater fight; if bad men appear, you will relieve the earth of the bad. Suppose then that I lose my life in this way. You will die a good man, doing a noble act. For since he must certainly die, of necessity a man must be found doing something, either following the employment of a husbandman, or digging, or trading, or serving in a consulship, or suffering from indigestion or from diarrhoea. What then do you wish to be doing when you are found by death? I, for my part, would wish to be found doing something which belongs to a man, beneficent, suitable to the general interest, noble. But if I cannot be found doing things so great, I would be found doing at least that which I cannot be hindered from doing, that which is permitted me to do, correcting myself, cultivating the faculty which makes use of appearances, laboring at freedom from the affects (laboring at tranquillity of mind); rendering to the relations of life their due. If I succeed so far, also (I would be found) touching on (advancing to) the third topic (or head) safety in forming judgments about things. If death surprises me when I am busy about these things, it is enough for me if I can stretch out my hands to God and say: The means which I have received from thee for seeing thy administration (of the world) and following it I have not neglected; I have not dishonored thee by my acts; see how I have used my perceptions, see how I have used my preconceptions; have I ever blamed thee? have I been discontented with anything that happens, or wished it to be otherwise? have I wished to transgress the (established) relations (of things)? That thou hast given me life, I thank thee for what thou hast given. So long as I have used the things which are thine I am content. Take them back and place them wherever thou mayest choose, for thine were all things, thou gavest them to me. Is it not enough to depart in this state of mind? and what life is better and more becoming than that of a man who is in this state of mind? and what end is more happy?

ABOUT PURITY (CLEANLINESS)

Some persons raise a question whether the social feeling is contained in the nature of man; and yet I think that these same persons would have no doubt that love of purity is certainly contained in it, and that if man is distinguished from other animals by anything, he is distinguished by this. When then we see any other animal cleaning itself, we are accustomed to speak of the act with surprise, and to add that the animal is acting like a man; and on the other hand, if a man blames an animal for being dirty, straightway, as if we were making an excuse for it, we say that of course the animal is not a human creature. So we suppose that there is something superior in man, and that we first receive it from the gods. For since the gods by their nature are pure and free from corruption, so far as men approach them by reason, so far do they cling to purity and to a love (habit) of purity. But since it is impossible that man's nature (Greek: *ousia*) can be altogether pure, being mixed (composed) of such materials, reason is applied, as far as it is possible, and reason endeavors to make human nature love purity.

The first then and highest purity is that which is in the soul; and we say the same of impurity. Now you could not discover the impurity of the soul as you could discover that of the body; but as to the soul, what else could you find in it than that which makes it filthy in respect to the acts which are her own? Now the acts of the soul are movement towards an object or movement from it, desire, aversion, preparation, design (purpose), assent. What then is it which in these acts makes the soul filthy and impure? Nothing else than her own bad judgments (Greek: *chrimata*). Consequently the impurity of the soul is the soul's bad opinions; and the purification of the soul is the planting in it of proper opinions; and the soul is pure which has proper opinions, for the soul alone in her own acts is free from perturbation and pollution.

For we ought not even by the appearance of the body to deter the multitude from philosophy; but as in other things, a philosopher should show himself cheerful and tranquil, so also he should in the things that relate to the body. See, ye men, that I have nothing, that I want nothing; see how I am without a house, and without a city, and an exile, if it happens to be so, and without a hearth I live more free from trouble and more happily than all of noble birth and than the rich. But look at my poor body also and observe that it is not injured by my hard way of living. But if a man says this to me, who has the appearance (dress) and face of a condemned man, what god shall persuade me to approach philosophy, if it makes men such persons? Far from it; I would not choose to do so, even if I were going to become a wise man. I indeed would rather that a young man, who is making his first movements towards philosophy, should come to me with his hair carefully trimmed than with it dirty and rough, for there is seen in him a certain notion (appearance) of beauty and a desire of (attempt at) that which is becoming; and where he supposes it to be, there also he strives that it shall be. It is only necessary to show him (what it is), and to say: Young man, you seek beauty, and you do well; you must know then that it (is produced) grows in that part of you where you have the rational faculty; seek it there where you have the movements towards and movements from things, where you have the desires towards and the aversion from things; for this is what you have in yourself of a superior kind; but the poor body is naturally only earth; why do you labor about it to no purpose? if you shall learn nothing else, you will learn from time that the body is nothing. But if a man comes to me daubed with filth, dirty, with a moustache down to his knees, what can I say to him, by what kind of resemblance can I lead him on? For about what has he busied himself which resembles beauty, that I may be able to change him and say, Beauty is not in this, but in that? Would you have me to tell him, that beauty consists not in being daubed with muck, but that it lies in the rational part? Has he any desire of beauty? has he any form of it in his mind? Go and talk to a hog, and tell him not to roll in the mud.

ON ATTENTION

When you have remitted your attention for a short time, do not imagine this, that you will recover it when you choose; but let this thought be present to you, that in consequence of the fault committed today your affairs must be in a worse condition for all that follows. For first, and what causes most trouble, a habit of not attending is formed in you; then a habit of deferring your attention. And continually from time to time you drive away by deferring it the happiness of life, proper behavior, the being and living conformably to nature. If then the procrastination of attention is profitable, the complete omission of attention is more profitable; but if it is not profitable, why do you not maintain your attention constant? Today I choose to play. Well then, ought you not to play with attention? I choose to sing. What then hinders you from doing so with attention? Is there any part of life excepted, to which attention does not extend? For will you do it (anything in life) worse by using attention, and better by not attending at all? And what else of the things in life is done better by those who do not use attention? Does he who works in wood work better by not attending to it? Does the captain of a ship manage it better by not attending? and are any of the smaller acts done better by inattention? Do you not see that when you have let your mind loose, it is no longer in your power to recall it, either to propriety, or to modesty, or to moderation; but you do everything that comes into your mind in obedience to your inclinations.

First then we ought to have these (rules) in readiness, and to do nothing without them, and we ought to keep the soul directed to this mark, to pursue nothing external, and nothing which belongs to others (or is in the power of others), but to do as he has appointed who has the power; we ought to pursue altogether the things which are in the power of the will, and all other things as it is permitted. Next to this we ought to remember who we are, and what is our name, and to endeavor to direct our duties towards the character (nature) of our several relations (in life) in this manner: what is the season for singing, what is the season for play, and in whose presence; what will be the consequence of the act; whether our associates will despise us, whether we shall despise them; when to jeer (Greek: *schopsai*), and whom to ridicule; and on what occasion to comply and with whom; and finally, in complying how to maintain our own character. But wherever you have deviated from any of these rules, there is damage immediately, not from anything external, but from the action itself.

What then? is it possible to be free from faults (if you do all this)? It is not possible; but this is possible, to direct your efforts incessantly to being faultless. For we must be content if by never remitting this attention we shall escape at least a few errors. But now when you have said, Tomorrow I will begin to attend, you must be told that you are saying this, Today I will be shameless, disregardful of time and place, mean; it will be in the power of others to give me pain; today I will be passionate and envious. See how many evil things you are permitting yourself to do. If it is good to use attention tomorrow, how much better is it to do so today? if tomorrow it is in your interest to attend, much more is it today, that you may be able to do so tomorrow also, and may not defer it again to the third day.

AGAINST OR TO THOSE WHO READILY TELL THEIR OWN AFFAIRS

When a man has seemed to us to have talked with simplicity (candor) about his own affairs, how is it that at last we are ourselves also induced to discover to him our own secrets and we think this to be candid behavior? In the first place, because it seems unfair for a man to have listened to the affairs of his neighbor, and not to communicate to him also in turn our own affairs; next, because we think that we shall not present to them the appearance of candid men when we are silent about our own affairs. Indeed, men are often accustomed to say, I have told you all my affairs, will you tell me nothing of your own? where is this done? Besides, we have also this opinion that we can safely trust him who has already told us his own affairs; for the notion rises in our mind that this man could never divulge our affairs because he would be cautious that we also should not divulge his. In this way also the incautious are caught by the soldiers at Rome. A soldier sits by you in a common dress and begins to speak ill of Caesar; then you, as if you had received a pledge of his fidelity by his having begun the abuse, utter yourself also what you think, and then you are carried off in chains.

Something of this kind happens to us also generally. Now as this man has confidently intrusted his affairs to me, shall I also do so to any man whom I meet? (No), for when I have heard, I keep silence, if I am of such a disposition; but he goes forth and tells all men what he has heard. Then, if I hear what has been done, if I be a man like him, I resolve to be revenged, I divulge what he has told me; I both disturb others, and am disturbed myself. But if I remember that one man does not injure another, and that every man's acts injure and profit him, I secure this, that I do not anything like him, but still I suffer what I do suffer through my own silly talk.

True, but it is unfair when you have heard the secrets of your neighbor for you in your turn to communicate nothing to him. Did I ask you for your secrets, my man? did you communicate your affairs on certain terms, that you should in return hear mine also? If you are a babbler and think that all who meet you are friends, do you wish me also to be like you? But why, if you did well in intrusting your affairs to me, and it is not well for me to intrust mine to you, do you wish me to be so rash? It is just the same as if I had a cask which is water-tight, and you one with a hole in it, and you should come and deposit with me your wine that I might put it into my cask, and then should complain that I also did not intrust my wine to you, for you have a cask with a hole in it. How then is there any equality here? You intrusted your affairs to a man who is faithful and modest, to a man who thinks that his own actions alone are injurious and (or) useful, and that nothing external is. Would you have me intrust mine to you, a man who has dishonored his own faculty of will, and who wishes to gain some small bit of money or some office or promotion in the court (emperor's palace), even if you should be going to murder your own children, like Medea? Where (in what) is this equality (fairness)? But show yourself to me to be faithful, modest, and steady; show me that you have friendly opinions; show that your cask has no hole in it; and you will see how I shall not wait for you to trust me with your own affairs, but I myself shall come to you and ask you to hear mine. For who does not choose to make use of a good vessel? Who does not value a benevolent and faithful adviser? Who will not willingly receive a man who is ready to bear a share, as we may say, of the difficulty of his circumstances, and by this very act to ease the burden, by taking a part of it.

THE ENCHIRIDION

I

Of things some are in our power, and others are not. In our power are opinion (Greek: *hupolaepsis*), movement towards a thing (Greek: *hormae*), desire, aversion (Greek: *echchlisis*), turning from a thing; and in a word, whatever are our acts. Not in our power are the body, property, reputation, offices (magisterial power), and in a word, whatever are not our own acts. And the things in our power are by nature free, not subject to restraint or hindrance; but the things not in our power are weak, slavish, subject to restraint, in the power of others. Remember then, that if you think the things which are by nature slavish to be free, and the things which are in the power of others to be your own, you will be hindered, you will lament, you will be disturbed, you will blame both gods and men; but if you think that only which is your own to be your own, and if you think that what is another's, as it really is, belongs to another, no man will ever compel you, no man will hinder you, you will never blame any man, you will accuse no man, you will do nothing involuntarily (against your will), no man will harm you, you will have no enemy, for you will not suffer any harm.

If then you desire (aim at) such great things remember that you must not (attempt to) lay hold of them with a small effort; but you must leave alone some things entirely, and postpone others for the present. But if you wish for these things also (such great things), and power (office) and wealth, perhaps you will not gain even these very things (power and wealth) because you aim also at those former things (such great things); certainly you will fail in those things through which alone happiness and freedom are secured. Straightway then practise saying to every harsh appearance: You are an appearance, and in no manner what you appear to be. Then examine it by the rules which you possess, and by this first and chiefly, whether it relates to the things which are in our power or to things which are not in our power; and if it relates to anything which is not in our power, be ready to say that it does not concern you.

II

Remember that desire contains in it the profession (hope) of obtaining that which you desire; and the profession (hope) in aversion (turning from a thing) is that you will not fall into that which you attempt to avoid; and he who fails in his desire is unfortunate; and he who falls into that which he would avoid is unhappy. If then you attempt to avoid only the things contrary to nature which are within your power you will not be involved in any of the things which you would avoid. But if you attempt to avoid disease, or death, or poverty, you will be unhappy. Take away then aversion from all things which are not in our power, and transfer it to the things contrary to nature which are in our power. But destroy desire completely for the present. For if you desire anything which is not in our power, you must be unfortunate; but of the things in our power, and which it would be good to desire, nothing yet is before you. But employ only the power of moving towards an object and retiring from it; and these powers indeed only slightly and with exceptions and with remission.

III

In everything which pleases the soul, or supplies a want, or is loved, remember to add this to the (description, notion): What is the nature of each thing, beginning from the smallest? If you love an earthen vessel, say it is an earthen vessel which you love; for when it has been broken you will not be disturbed. If you are kissing your child or wife, say that it is a human being whom you are kissing, for when the wife or child dies you will not be disturbed.

IV

When you are going to take in hand any act remind yourself what kind of an act it is. If you are going to bathe, place before yourself what happens in the bath; some splashing the water, others pushing against one another, others abusing one another, and some stealing; and thus with more safety you will undertake the matter, if you say to yourself, I now intend to bathe, and to maintain my will in a manner conformable to nature. And so you will do in every act; for thus if any hindrance to bathing shall happen let this thought be ready. It was not this only that I intended, but I intended also to maintain my will in a way conformable to nature; but I shall not maintain it so if I am vexed at what happens.

V

Men are disturbed not by the things which happen, but by the opinions about the things; for example, death is nothing terrible, for if it were it would have seemed so to Socrates; for the opinion about death that it is terrible, is the terrible thing. When then we are impeded, or disturbed, or grieved, let us never blame others, but ourselves—that is, our opinions. It is the act of an ill-instructed man to blame others for his own bad condition; it is the act of one who has begun to be instructed, to lay the blame on himself; and of one whose instruction is completed, neither to blame another, nor himself.

VI

Be not elated at any advantage (excellence) which belongs to another. If a horse when he is elated should say, I am beautiful, one might endure it. But when you are elated, and say, I have a beautiful horse, you must know that you are elated at having a good horse. What then is your own? The use of appearances. Consequently when in the use of appearances you are conformable to nature, then be elated, for then you will be elated at something good which is your own.

VII

As on a voyage when the vessel has reached a port, if you go out to get water it is an amusement by the way to pick up a shellfish or some bulb, but your thoughts ought to be directed to the ship, and you ought to be constantly watching if the captain should call, and then you must throw away all those things, that you may not be bound and pitched into the ship like sheep. So in life also, if there be given to you instead of a little bulb and a shell a wife and child, there will be nothing to prevent (you from taking them). But if the captain should call, run to the ship and leave all those things without regard to them. But if you are old, do not even go far from the ship, lest when you are called you make default.

VIII

Seek not that the things which happen should happen as you wish; but wish the things which happen to be as they are, and you will have a tranquil flow of life.

IX

Disease is an impediment to the body, but not to the will, unless the will itself chooses. Lameness is an impediment to the leg, but not to the will. And add this reflection on the occasion of everything that happens; for you will find it an impediment to something else, but not to yourself.

X

On the occasion of every accident (event) that befalls you, remember to turn to yourself and inquire what power you have for turning it to use. If you see a fair man or a fair woman, you will find that the power to resist is temperance (continence). If labor (pain) be presented to you, you will find that it is endurance. If it be abusive words, you will find it to be patience. And if you have been thus formed to the (proper) habit, the appearances will not carry you along with them.

XI

Never say about anything, I have lost it, but say I have restored it. Is your child dead? It has been restored. Is your wife dead? She has been restored. Has your estate been taken from you? Has not then this also been restored? But he who has taken it from me is a bad man. But what is it to you, by whose hands the giver demanded it back? So long as he may allow you, take care of it as a thing which belongs to another, as travellers do with their inn.

XII

If you intend to improve, throw away such thoughts as these: if I neglect my affairs, I shall not have the means of living: unless I chastise my slave, he will be bad. For it is better to die of hunger and so to be released from grief and fear than to live in abundance with perturbation; and it is better for your slave to be bad than for you to be unhappy. Begin then from little things. Is the oil spilled? Is a little wine stolen? Say on the occasion, at such price is sold freedom from perturbation; at such price is sold tranquillity, but nothing is got for nothing. And when you call your slave, consider that it is possible that he does not hear; and if he does hear, that he will do nothing which you wish. But matters are not so well with him, but altogether well with you, that it should be in his power for you to be not disturbed.

XIII

If you would improve, submit to be considered without sense and foolish with respect to externals. Wish to be considered to know nothing; and if you shall seem to some to be a person of importance, distrust yourself. For you should know that it is not easy both to keep your will in a condition conformable to nature and (to secure) external things: but if a man is careful about the one, it is an absolute necessity that he will neglect the other.

XIV

If you would have your children and your wife and your friends to live for ever, you are silly; for you would have the things which are not in your power to be in your power, and the things which belong to others to be yours. So if you would have your slave to be free from faults, you are a fool; for you would have badness not to be badness, but something else. But if you wish not to fail in your desires, you are able to do that. Practise then this which you are able to do. He is the master of every man who has the power over the things which another person wishes or does not wish, the power to confer them on him or to take them away. Whoever then wishes to be free let him neither wish for anything nor avoid anything which depends on others: if he does not observe this rule, he must be a slave.

XV

Remember that in life you ought to behave as at a banquet. Suppose that something is carried round and is opposite to you. Stretch out your hand and take a portion with decency. Suppose that it passes by you. Do not detain it. Suppose that it is not yet come to you. Do not send your desire forward to it, but wait till it is opposite to you. Do so with respect to children, so with respect to a wife, so with respect to magisterial offices, so with respect to wealth, and you will be some time a worthy partner of the banquets of the gods. But if you take none of the things which are set before you, and even despise them, then you will be not only a fellow banqueter with the gods, but also a partner with them in power. For by acting thus Diogenes and Heracleitus and those like them were deservedly divine, and were so called.

XVI

When you see a person weeping in sorrow either when a child goes abroad or when he is dead, or when the man has lost his property, take care that the appearance do not hurry you away with it, as if he were suffering in external things. But straightway make a distinction in your own mind, and be in readiness to say, it is not that which has happened that afflicts this man, for it does not afflict another, but it is the opinion about this thing which afflicts the man. So far as words then do not be unwilling to show him sympathy, and even if it happens so, to lament with him. But take care that you do not lament internally also.

XVII

Remember that thou art an actor in a play, of such a kind as the teacher (author) may choose; if short, of a short one; if long, of a long one: if he wishes you to act the part of a poor man, see that you act the part naturally; if the part of a lame man, of a magistrate, of a private person, (do the same). For this is your duty, to act well the part that is given to you; but to select the part, belongs to another.

XVIII

When a raven has croaked inauspiciously, let not the appearance hurry you away with it; but straightway make a distinction in your mind and say, None of these things is signified to me, but either to my poor body, or to my small property, or to my reputation, or to my children, or to my wife: but to me all significations are auspicious if I choose. For whatever of these things results, it is in my power to derive benefit from it.

XIX

You can be invincible, if you enter into no contest in which it is not in your power to conquer. Take care then when you observe a man honored before others or possessed of great power or highly esteemed for any reason, not to suppose him happy, and be not carried away by the appearance. For if the nature of the good is in our power, neither envy nor jealousy will have a place in us. But you yourself will not wish to be a general or senator (Greek: *prutanis*) or consul, but a free man: and there is only one way to this, to despise (care not for) the things which are not in our power.

XX

Remember that it is not he who reviles you or strikes you, who insults you, but it is your opinion about these things as being insulting. When then a man irritates you, you must know that it is your own opinion which has irritated you. Therefore especially try not to be carried away by the appearance. For if you once gain time and delay, you will more easily master yourself.

XXI

Let death and exile and every other thing which appears dreadful be daily before your eyes; but most of all death: and you will never think of anything mean nor will you desire anything extravagantly.

XXII

If you desire philosophy, prepare yourself from the beginning to be ridiculed, to expect that many will sneer at you, and say, He has all at once returned to us as a philosopher; and whence does he get this supercilious look for us? Do you not show a supercilious look; but hold on to the things which seem to you best as one appointed by God to this station. And remember that if you abide in the same principles, these men who first ridiculed will afterwards admire you; but if you shall have been overpowered by them, you will bring on yourself double ridicule.

XXIII

If it should ever happen to you to be turned to externals in order to please some person, you must know that you have lost your purpose in life. Be satisfied then in everything with being a philosopher; and if you wish to seem also to any person to be a philosopher, appear so to yourself, and you will be able to do this.

XXIV

Let not these thoughts afflict you, I shall live unhonored and be nobody nowhere. For if want of honor (Greek: *atimia*) is an evil, you cannot be in evil through the means (fault) of another any more than you can be involved in anything base. Is it then your business to obtain the rank of a magistrate, or to be received at a banquet? By no means. How then can this be want of honor (dishonor)? And how will you be nobody nowhere, when you ought to be somebody in those things only which are in your power, in which indeed it is permitted to you to be a man of the greatest worth? But your friends will be without assistance! What do you mean by being without assistance? They will not receive money from you, nor will you make them Roman citizens. Who then told you that these are among the things which are in our power, and not in the power of others? And who can give to another what he has not himself? Acquire money then, your friends say, that we also may have something. If I can acquire money and also keep myself modest and faithful and magnanimous, point out the way, and I will acquire it. But if you ask me to lose the things which are good and my own, in order that you may gain the things which are not good, see how unfair and silly you are. Besides, which would you rather have, money or a faithful and modest friend? For this end then rather help me to be such a man, and do not ask me to do this by which I shall lose that character. But my country, you say, as far as it depends on me, will be without my help. I ask again, what help do you mean? It will not have porticos or baths through you. And what does this mean? For it is not furnished with shoes by means of a smith, nor with arms by means of a shoemaker. But it is enough if every man fully discharges the work that is his own: and if you provided it with another citizen faithful and modest, would you not be useful to it? Yes. Then you also cannot be useless to it. What place then, you say, shall I hold in the city? Whatever you can, if you maintain at the same time your fidelity and modesty. But if when you wish to be useful to the state, you shall lose these qualities, what profit could you be to it, if you were made shameless and faithless?

XXV

Has any man been preferred before you at a banquet, or in being saluted, or in being invited to a consultation? If these things are good, you ought to rejoice that he has obtained them; but if bad, be not grieved because you have not obtained them. And remember that you cannot, if you do not the same things in order to obtain what is not in our own power, be considered worthy of the same (equal) things. For how can a man obtain an equal share with another when he does not visit a man's doors as that other man does; when he does not attend him when he goes abroad, as the other man does; when he does not praise (flatter) him as another does? You will be unjust then and insatiable, if you do not part with the price, in return for which those things are sold, and if you wish to obtain them for nothing. Well, what is the price of lettuces? An obolus perhaps. If then a man gives up the obolus, and receives the lettuces, and if you do not give up the obolus and do not obtain the lettuces, do not suppose that you receive less than he who has got the lettuces; for as he has the lettuces, so you have the obolus which you did not give. In the same way then in the other matter also you have not been invited to a man's feast, for you did not give to the host the price at which the supper is sold; but he sells it for praise (flattery), he sells it for personal attention. Give then the price, if it is for your interest, for which it is sold. But if you wish both not to give the price and to obtain the things, you are insatiable and silly. Have you nothing then in place of the supper? You have indeed, you have the not flattering of him, whom you did not choose to flatter; you have the not enduring of the man when he enters the room.

XXVI

We may learn the wish (will) of nature from the things in which we do not differ from one another: for instance, when your neighbor's slave has broken his cup, or anything else, we are ready to say forthwith, that it is one of the things which happen. You must know then that when your cup also is broken, you ought to think as you did when your neighbor's cup was broken. Transfer this reflection to greater things also. Is another man's child or wife dead? There is no one who would not say, This is an event incident to man. But when a man's own child or wife is dead, forthwith he calls out, Woe to me, how wretched I am! But we ought to remember how we feel when we hear that it has happened to others.

XXVII

As a mark is not set up for the purpose of missing the aim, so neither does the nature of evil exist in the world.

XXVIII

If any person was intending to put your body in the power of any man whom you fell in with on the way, you would be vexed; but that you put your understanding in the power of any man whom you meet, so that if he should revile you, it is disturbed and troubled, are you not ashamed at this?

XXIX

In every act observe the things which come first, and those which follow it; and so proceed to the act. If you do not, at first you will approach it with alacrity, without having thought of the things which will follow; but afterwards, when certain base (ugly) things have shown themselves, you will be ashamed. A man wishes to conquer at the Olympic games. I also wish indeed, for it is a fine thing. But observe both the things which come first, and the things which follow; and then begin the act. You must do everything according to rule, eat according to strict orders, abstain from delicacies, exercise yourself as you are bid at appointed times, in heat, in cold, you must not drink cold water, nor wine as you choose; in a word, you must deliver yourself up to the exercise master as you do to the physician, and then proceed to the contest. And sometimes you will strain the hand, put the ankle out of joint, swallow much dust, sometimes be flogged, and after all this be defeated. When you have considered all this, if you still choose, go to the contest: if you do not you will behave like children, who at one time play at wrestlers, another time as flute players, again as gladiators, then as trumpeters, then as tragic actors. So you also will be at one time an athlete, at another a gladiator, then a rhetorician, then a philosopher, but with your whole soul you will be nothing at all; but like an ape you imitate everything that you see, and one thing after another pleases you. For you have not undertaken anything with consideration, nor have you surveyed it well; but carelessly and with cold desire. Thus some who have seen a philosopher and having heard one speak, as Euphrates speaks—and who can speak as he does?—they wish to be philosophers themselves also. My man, first of all consider what kind of thing it is; and then examine your own nature, if you are able to sustain the character. Do you wish to be a pentathlete or a wrestler? Look at your arms, your thighs, examine your loins. For different men are formed by nature for different things. Do you think that if you do these things, you can eat in the same manner, drink in the same manner, and in the same manner loathe certain things? You must pass sleepless nights, endure toil, go away from your kinsmen, be despised by a slave, in everything have the inferior part, in honor, in office, in the courts of justice, in every little matter. Consider these things, if you would exchange for them, freedom from passions, liberty, tranquillity. If not, take care that, like little children, you be not now a philosopher, then a servant of the publicani, then a rhetorician, then a procurator (manager) for Caesar. These things are not consistent. You must be one man, either good or bad. You must either cultivate your own ruling faculty, or external things. You must either exercise your skill on internal things or on external things; that is you must either maintain the position of a philosopher or that of a common person.

XXX

Duties are universally measured by relations (Greek: *tais schsesi*). Is a man a father? The precept is to take care of him, to yield to him in all things, to submit when he is reproachful, when he inflicts blows. But suppose that he is a bad father. Were you then by nature made akin to a good father? No; but to a father. Does a brother wrong you? Maintain then your own position towards him, and do not examine what he is doing, but what you must do that your will shall be conformable to nature. For another will not damage you, unless you choose: but you will be damaged then when you shall think that you are damaged. In this way then you will discover your duty from the relation of a neighbor, from that of a citizen, from that of a general, if you are accustomed to contemplate the relations.

XXXI

As to piety towards the gods you must know that this is the chief thing, to have right opinions about them, to think that they exist, and that they administer the All well and justly; and you must fix yourself in this principle (duty), to obey them, and to yield to them in everything which happens, and voluntarily to follow it as being accomplished by the wisest intelligence. For if you do so, you will never either blame the gods, nor will you accuse them of neglecting you. And it is not possible for this to be done in any other way than by withdrawing from the things which are not in our power, and by placing the good and the evil only in those things which are in our power. For if you think that any of the things which are not in our power is good or bad, it is absolutely necessary that, when you do not obtain what you wish, and when you fall into those things which you do not wish, you will find fault and hate those who are the cause of them; for every animal is formed by nature to this, to fly from and to turn from the things which appear harmful and the things which are the cause of the harm, but to follow and admire the things which are useful and the causes of the useful. It is impossible then for a person who thinks that he is harmed to be delighted with that which he thinks to be the cause of the harm, as it is also impossible to be pleased with the harm itself. For this reason also a father is reviled by his son, when he gives no part to his son of the things which are considered to be good; and it was this which made Polynices and Eteocles enemies, the opinion that royal power was a good. It is for this reason that the cultivator of the earth reviles the gods, for this reason the sailor does, and the merchant, and for this reason those who lose their wives and their children. For where the useful (your interest) is, there also piety is. Consequently he who takes care to desire as he ought and to avoid (Greek: *echchlinein*) as he ought, at the same time also cares after piety. But to make libations and to sacrifice and to offer first-fruits according to the custom of our fathers, purely and not meanly nor carelessly nor scantily nor above our ability, is a thing which belongs to all to do.

XXXII

When you have recourse to divination, remember that you do not know how it will turn out, but that you are come to inquire from the diviner. But of what kind it is, you know when you come, if indeed you are a philosopher. For if it is any of the things which are not in our power, it is absolutely necessary that it must be neither good nor bad. Do not then bring to the diviner desire or aversion (Greek: *echchlinein*): if you do, you will approach him with fear. But having determined in your mind that everything which shall turn out (result) is indifferent, and does not concern you, and whatever it may be, for it will be in your power to use it well, and no man will hinder this, come then with confidence to the gods as your advisers. And then when any advice shall have been given, remember whom you have taken as advisers, and whom you will have neglected, if you do not obey them. And go to divination, as Socrates said that you ought, about those matters in which all the inquiry has reference to the result, and in which means are not given either by reason nor by any other art for knowing the thing which is the subject of the inquiry. Wherefore when we ought to share a friend's danger, or that of our country, you must not consult the diviner whether you ought to share it. For even if the diviner shall tell you that the signs of the victims are unlucky, it is plain that this is a token of death, or mutilation of part of the body, or of exile. But reason prevails, that even with these risks, we should share the dangers of our friend, and of our country. Therefore attend to the greater diviner, the Pythian god, who ejected from the temple him who did not assist his friend, when he was being murdered.

XXXIII

Immediately prescribe some character and some form to yourself, which you shall observe both when you are alone and when you meet with men.

And let silence be the general rule, or let only what is necessary be said, and in few words. And rarely, and when the occasion calls, we shall say something; but about none of the common subjects, not about gladiators, nor horse-races, nor about athletes, nor about eating or drinking, which are the usual subjects; and especially not about men, as blaming them or praising them, or comparing them. If then you are able, bring over by your conversation, the conversation of your associates, to that which is proper; but if you should happen to be confined to the company of strangers, be silent.

Let not your laughter be much, nor on many occasions, nor excessive.

Refuse altogether to take an oath, if it is possible; if it is not, refuse as far as you are able.

Avoid banquets which are given by strangers and by ignorant persons. But if ever there is occasion to join in them, let your attention be carefully fixed, that you slip not into the manners of the vulgar (the uninstructed). For you must know, that if your companion be impure, he also who keeps company with him must become impure, though he should happen to be pure.

Take (apply) the things which relate to the body as far as the bare use, as food, drink, clothing, house, and slaves; but exclude everything which is for show or luxury.

As to pleasure with women, abstain as far as you can before marriage; but if you do indulge in it, do it in the way which is conformable to custom. Do not however be disagreeable to those who indulge in these pleasures, or reprove them; and do not often boast that you do not indulge in them yourself.

If a man has reported to you, that a certain person speaks ill of you, do not make any defence (answer) to what has been told you; but reply, The man did not know the rest of my faults, for he would not have mentioned these only.

It is not necessary to go to the theatres often: but if there is ever a proper occasion for going, do not show yourself as being a partisan of any man except yourself, that is, desire only that to be done which is done, and for him only to gain the prize who gains the prize; for in this way you will meet with no hindrance. But abstain entirely from shouts and laughter at any (thing or person), or violent emotions. And when you are come away, do not talk much about what has passed on the stage, except about that which may lead to your own improvement. For it is plain, if you do talk much, that you admired the spectacle (more than you ought).

Do not go to the hearing of certain persons' recitations, nor visit them readily. But if you do attend, observe gravity and sedateness, and also avoid making yourself disagreeable.

When you are going to meet with any person, and particularly one of those who are considered to be in a superior condition, place before yourself what Socrates or Zeno would have done in such circumstances, and you will have no difficulty in making a proper use of the occasion.

When you are going to any of those who are in great power, place before yourself that you will not find the man at home, that you will be excluded, that the door will not be opened to you, that the man will not care about you. And if with all this it is your duty to visit him, bear what happens, and never say to yourself that it was not worth the trouble. For this is silly, and marks the character of a man who is offended by externals.

In company take care not to speak much and excessively about your own acts or dangers; for as it is pleasant to you to make mention of your own dangers, it is not so pleasant to others to hear what has happened to you. Take care also not to provoke laughter; for this is a slippery way towards vulgar habits, and is also adapted to diminish the respect of your neighbors. It is a dangerous habit also to approach obscene talk. When then, anything of this kind happens, if there is a good opportunity, rebuke the man who has proceeded to this talk; but if there is not an opportunity, by your silence at least, and blushing and expression of dissatisfaction by your countenance, show plainly that you are displeased at such talk.

XXXIV

If you have received the impression (Greek: *phantasion*) of any pleasure, guard yourself against being carried away by it; but let the thing wait for you, and allow yourself a certain delay on your own part. Then think of both times, of the time when you will enjoy the pleasure, and of the time after the enjoyment of the pleasure, when you will repent and will reproach yourself. And set against these things how you will rejoice, if you have abstained from the pleasure, and how you will commend yourself. But if it seem to you seasonable to undertake (do) the thing, take care that the charm of it, and the pleasure, and the attraction of it shall not conquer you; but set on the other side the consideration, how much better it is to be conscious that you have gained this victory.

XXXV

When you have decided that a thing ought to be done, and are doing it, never avoid being seen doing it, though the many shall form an unfavorable opinion about it. For if it is not right to do it, avoid doing the thing; but if it is right, why are you afraid of those who shall find fault wrongly?

XXXVI

As the proposition, it is either day, or it is night, is of great importance for the disjunctive argument, but for the conjunctive, is of no value, so in a symposium (entertainment) to select the larger share is of great value for the body, but for the maintenance of the social feeling is worth nothing. When, then, you are eating with another, remember, to look not only to the value for the body of the things set before you, but also to the value of the behavior towards the host which ought to be observed.

XXXVII

If you have assumed a character above your strength, you have both acted in this manner in an unbecoming way, and you have neglected that which you might have fulfilled.

XXXVIII

In walking about, as you take care not to step on a nail, or to sprain your foot, so take care not to damage your own ruling faculty; and if we observe this rule in every act, we shall undertake this act with more security.

XXXIX

The measure of possession (property) is to every man the body, as the foot is of the shoe. If then you stand on this rule (the demands of the body), you will maintain the measure; but if you pass beyond it, you must then of necessity be hurried as it were down a precipice. As also in the matter of the shoe, if you go beyond the (necessities of the) foot, the shoe is gilded, then of a purple color, then embroidered; for there is no limit to that which has once passed the true measure.

XL

Women forthwith from the age of fourteen are called by the men mistresses (Greek: *churiai, dominae*). Therefore, since they see that there is nothing else that they can obtain, but only the power of lying with men, they begin to decorate themselves, and to place all their hopes in this. It is worth our while then to take care that they may know that they are valued (by men) for nothing else than appearing (being) decent and modest and discreet.

XLI

It is a mark of a mean capacity to spend much time on the things which concern the body, such as much exercise, much eating, much drinking, much easing of the body, much copulation. But these things should be done as subordinate things; and let all your care be directed to the mind.

XLII

When any person treats you ill or speaks ill of you, remember that he does this or says this because he thinks that it is his duty. It is not possible then for him to follow that which seems right to you, but that which seems right to himself. Accordingly if he is wrong in his opinion, he is the person who is hurt, for he is the person who has been deceived; for if a man shall suppose the true conjunction to be false, it is not the conjunction which is hindered, but the man who has been deceived about it. If you proceed then from these opinions, you will be mild in temper to him who reviles you; for say on each occasion, It seemed so to him.

XLIII

Everything has two handles, the one by which it may be borne, the other by which it may not. If your brother acts unjustly, do not lay hold of the act by that handle wherein he acts unjustly, for this is the handle which cannot be borne; but lay hold of the other, that he is your brother, that he was nurtured with you, and you will lay hold of the thing by that handle by which it can be borne.

XLIV

These reasonings do not cohere: I am richer than you, therefore I am better than you; I am more eloquent than you, therefore I am better than you. On the contrary, these rather cohere: I am richer than you, therefore my possessions are greater than yours; I am more eloquent than you, therefore my speech is superior to yours. But you are neither possession nor speech.

XLV

Does a man bathe quickly (early)? do not say that he bathes badly, but that he bathes quickly. Does a man drink much wine? do not say that he does this badly, but say that he drinks much. For before you shall have determined the opinion how do you know whether he is acting wrong? Thus it will not happen to you to comprehend some appearances which are capable of being comprehended, but to assent to others.

XLVI

On no occasion call yourself a philosopher, and do not speak much among the uninstructed about theorems (philosophical rules, precepts); but do that which follows from them. For example, at a banquet do not say how a man ought to eat, but eat as you ought to eat. For remember that in this way Socrates also altogether avoided ostentation. Persons used to come to him and ask to be recommended by him to philosophers, and he used to take them to philosophers, so easily did he submit to being overlooked. Accordingly, if any conversation should arise among uninstructed persons about any theorem, generally be silent; for there is great danger that you will immediately vomit up what you have not digested. And when a man shall say to you that you know nothing, and you are not vexed, then be sure that you have begun the work (of philosophy). For even sheep do not vomit up their grass and show to the shepherds how much they have eaten; but when they have internally digested the pasture, they produce externally wool and milk. Do you also show not your theorems to the uninstructed, but show the acts which come from their digestion.

XLVII

When at a small cost you are supplied with everything for the body, do not be proud of this; nor, if you drink water, say on every occasion, I drink water. But consider first how much more frugal the poor are than we, and how much more enduring of labor. And if you ever wish to exercise yourself in labor and endurance, do it for yourself, and not for others. Do not embrace statues; but if you are ever very thirsty, take a draught of cold water and spit it out, and tell no man.

XLVIII

The condition and characteristic of an uninstructed person is this: he never expects from himself profit (advantage) nor harm, but from externals. The condition and characteristic of a philosopher is this: he expects all advantage and all harm from himself. The signs (marks) of one who is making progress are these: he censures no man, he praises no man, he blames no man, he accuses no man, he says nothing about himself as if he were somebody or knew something; when he is impeded at all or hindered, he blames himself; if a man praises him he ridicules the praiser to himself; if a man censures him he makes no defence; he goes about like weak persons, being careful not to move any of the things which are placed, before they are firmly fixed; he removes all desire from himself, and he transfers aversion (Greek: *echchlisin*) to those things only of the things within our power which are contrary to nature; he employs a moderate movement towards everything; whether he is considered foolish or ignorant he cares not; and in a word he watches himself as if he were an enemy and lying in ambush.

XLIX

When a man is proud because he can understand and explain the writings of Chrysippus, say to yourself, If Chrysippus had not written obscurely, this man would have had nothing to be proud of. But what is it that I wish? To understand nature and to follow it. I inquire therefore who is the interpreter? and when I have heard that it is Chrysippus, I come to him (the interpreter). But I do not understand what is written, and therefore I seek the interpreter. And so far there is yet nothing to be proud of. But when I shall have found the interpreter, the thing that remains is to use the precepts (the lessons). This itself is the only thing to be proud of. But if I shall admire the exposition, what else have I been made unless a grammarian instead of a philosopher? except in one thing, that I am explaining Chrysippus instead of Homer. When, then, any man says to me, Read Chrysippus to me, I rather blush, when I cannot show my acts like to and consistent with his words.

L

Whatever things (rules) are proposed to you (for the conduct of life) abide by them, as if they were laws, as if you would be guilty of impiety if you transgressed any of them. And whatever any man shall say about you, do not attend to it; for this is no affair of yours. How long will you then still defer thinking yourself worthy of the best things, and in no matter transgressing the distinctive reason? Have you accepted the theorems (rules), which it was your duty to agree to, and have you agreed to them? what teacher then do you still expect that you defer to him the correction of yourself? You are no longer a youth, but already a full-grown man. If, then, you are negligent and slothful, and are continually making procrastination after procrastination, and proposal (intention) after proposal, and fixing day after day, after which you will attend to yourself, you will not know that you are not making improvement, but you will continue ignorant (uninstructed) both while you live and till you die. Immediately then think it right to live as a full-grown man, and one who is making proficiency, and let everything which appears to you to be the best be to you a law which must not be transgressed. And if anything laborious or pleasant or glorious or inglorious be presented to you, remember that now is the contest, now are the Olympic games, and they cannot be deferred; and that it depends on one defeat and one giving way that progress is either lost or maintained. Socrates in this way became perfect, in all things improving himself, attending to nothing except to reason. But you, though you are not yet a Socrates, ought to live as one who wishes to be a Socrates.

LI

The first and most necessary place (part, Greek: *topos*) in philosophy is the use of theorems (precepts, Greek: *theoraemata*), for instance, that we must not lie; the second part is that of demonstrations, for instance, How is it proved that we ought not to lie? The third is that which is confirmatory of these two, and explanatory, for example, How is this a demonstration? For what is demonstration, what is consequence, what is contradiction, what is truth, what is falsehood? The third part (topic) is necessary on account of the second, and the second on account of the first; but the most necessary and that on which we ought to rest is the first. But we do the contrary. For we spend our time on the third topic, and all our earnestness is about it; but we entirely neglect the first. Therefore we lie; but the demonstration that we ought not to lie we have ready to hand.

LII

In every thing (circumstance) we should hold these maxims ready to hand:

Lead me, O Zeus, and thou O Destiny,
The way that I am bid by you to go:
To follow I am ready. If I choose not,
I make myself a wretch, and still must follow.

But whoso nobly yields unto necessity,
We hold him wise, and skill'd in things divine.

And the third also: O Crito, if so it pleases the gods, so let it be; Anytus and Melitus are able indeed to kill me, but they cannot harm me.